BUILD YOUR OWN

AI

A Beginner's Guide to Build Your First Intelligent System Highlight the A-Z aspect, indicating a comprehensive approach

By

Roronoa Hatake

TABLE OF CONTENTS

WHY AI

Well the reason for this cyber is this is my third time regarding this project and I get so excited about these things and it just goes over like blows over 10 minutes or 20 minutes so I decided to limit myself to five minutes to get you excited about this course and why it's the best time to be in a job.

So let's dive into a good four and a half minutes left. Why? Well we've all heard about applications of artificial intelligence that are popping up around us self-driving cars and heavy machinery. The list just keeps going on and on and on. But why right now why not 10 years ago not ten years later. Well the answer is hidden in this current which is called Moore's Law. It was originally identified in 1965 or more and what it says is that the power of the average computer is like in very simple terms the power of the average computer which you can buy for a thousand dollars will double every 18 to 24 months. And that's been as easy as the law has held and through good times and bad. War and Peace and the recession depressions and nothing stops this. And we've already surpassed the brain of an insect for another computer that was going for a thousand bucks. We're sitting at about the speed of the processing power of the brain of Rat by 2025 will be at the brain of a human. As you can see it's exponentially growing. And so this is a great time to be in artificial televisions. It's just going to be doubling the power every time or every three minutes. So some of my favorite examples are related to games like chess and go. So in 1997 deep mind was the first computer to beat Gary Kasparov in chess.

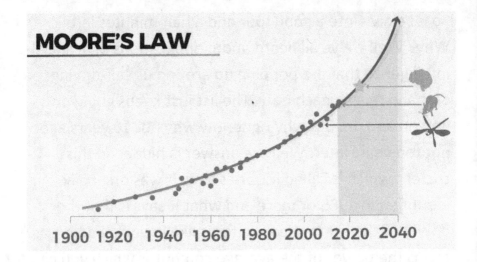

MOORE'S LAW

It was a huge thing, like one of the most broadcasted chess games on the planet ever. And at the same time. So that was like considering it an impossible feat right now on any phone you can install at chess which no human player will ever be. Because computers are that good. Now you just cannot beat a computer in Chesapeake put on the hardest setting and then just recently in Marsch doesn't succeed. A computer won against the 18 World times champion and world champion of the game of Go. Lisa Idole again considered it an impossible feat even at the start of the match. It was considered to be impossible that it's only going to happen 10 years from then but it happened. And by the way if you'd like to find out a bit more about the game. It's very very exciting and very interesting. It's got 40 media players. The thousand year old game is very popular in China, Japan and Korea. And it's much more complex than chess so it's just that there's many more possible combinations. So again something I would consider impossible is happening and it's happening now and much earlier than it's time. So how are we going for time? One minute 50 seconds. So that's what you'll see from this course. You'll see that we're using games to train AI. Why are we doing that? Because games are a confined environment where we can beat a game using artificial intelligence, then we can use the same principles to apply to business. And that's the exact same thing that the team at Google deep mine who created Alpha go who wants to get these adults. That's exactly what they did. They applied artificial intelligence to Google's warehouse to control the air cooling.

Why AI?

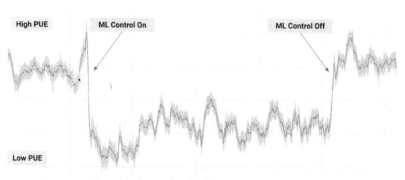

Source: https://deepmind.com/blog/deepmind-ai-reduces-google-data-centre-cooling-bill-40/

And what they found is that the electricity bill is a consumption you can see like it's going like this. As soon as they switch on the AI goes down. And then they switch it back off and go up. They were able to save 40 percent on their electricity bill and I have one that is 40 percent so you can find the full article on the deep mine blog. That is insane. Imagine that for a company of Google's scale which has millions and millions of servers. So there you go. That's that your connection between applying artificial intelligence and games and applying it to business is very very closely related. And that's what you will be able to do after this course. And finally one of my favorite blogs. Wait but why dot com. Check it out. Amazing blog by Tim Urban. This is how he describes the situation we're in. This is us and technological progress.

Why AI?

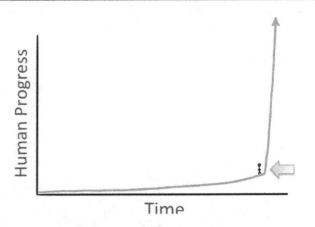

We're sitting here. This is what it looks like looks very very linear but because it's an exponential boom. This is what's going to happen in the next two years and there's very strong evidence from the things we see to suggest that we're sitting right over here and they can occur. And that my friends in-shore is why it's so exciting to be alive right now. Why is it so exciting to be and get into and be in the space of artificial intelligence because the power you have, the locations that you will be able to create or the ways you will be able to have what is going to be intense and insane. And I can't wait to see the first of all the scores. Let's get this started.

PLAN OF ATTACK

Today we're going to discuss the plan of attack for the section we're talking about kill learning. And we've got quite a few projects so I think it is a good idea for us to quickly go through them to understand what to expect in the upcoming videos. So here we go. All right. What we will learn in this section. First things first we will talk about what reinforcement learning actually is and what the philosophy behind reinforcement learning is and how reinforcement learning actually can be seen in real life and how it relates to things that we observe in real life are actually things that we do ourselves. They don't talk about the bellman equation, a very fundamental concept underpinning everything or a lot of things that are happening and for reinforcement learning especially in the space of CULE learning and what we're going to be discussing in this section of the course and in the following sections. Then we'll talk about the plan and the plan that raw iron artificial intelligence comes up with in order to navigate inside environments. We'll see how that comes together very quickly but quite interesting. There we'll talk about market of decision processes and your concept we're going to introduce a very new concept which will slowly even add a layer of sophistication to our Bellman equation to our whole reinforcement learning to our CULE learning concepts and that's the way this section is structured that we introduce the Bollmann equation a very simplistic form and then slowly throughout the projects we adds layers of sophistication to it in order to get to the final version. That is our designated destination in terms of Hillary but we'll get there slowly.

Plan of Attack

What we will learn in this section:
- What is Reinforcement Learning?
- The Bellman Equation
- The "Plan"
- Markov Decision Process (MDP)
- Policy vs Plan
- Adding a "Living Penalty"
- Q-Learning Intuition
- Temporal Difference
- Q-Learning Visualization

In order for us to have enough time to process all that information and let it settle in. And the mark of dissident prose is an extra layer of sophistication on top of what we've discussed or what we will have or if it is discussed by then there will be talk about policies versus plans. Another interesting Tauriel, they're all interesting. Just another quick project on how policy is different from plans and what the differences there are and these are terms that you will probably hear or read in the literature if you're going to be delving into it to get additional information on reinforcement learning. They're all talking about adding a living penalty to our environments. And that's kind of another way of adding complexity into the environments that our agents are going to be operating in. They're all talking about the intuition behind keep learning so up until that project we're going to be talking about values of states. And then finally we're going to switch to talking about values or actions or cube values and then we're going to introduce the temporal difference. This is a project where everything that we've learned is going to come together to explain how exactly agents or artificial intelligence learn how it updates its values through all the iterative process that it is going through. And then finally we're going to look at a visible zation of learning so we're going to take everything we learn and we're going to look at it happen in front of our eyes and watch an artificial intelligence actually perform CULE learning and do all the things that we're going to discuss on an intuitive level is going to actually do in practice and that will help us even further grasp that knowledge that we're going to be coming off in the section. So hopefully you're very excited about these upcoming projects. I definitely am. And there are some very interesting slides coming up and more importantly the concepts themselves are very very interesting and I'm sure you're going to enjoy them quite a lot. And I look forward to seeing you next time.

WHAT IS REINFORCEMENT LEARNING

I hope you're excited about today's project because we are taking our very first step into the world of the I. And today we're talking about reinforcement learning. It's a very important story because it will underpin everything else that is going to happen in this course. So let's get started here. We've got a little maze and this maze is our representation of an environment and that's what we're going to be dealing with in this course. We're going to be dealing with certain environments in which our artificial intelligence is going to be performing. It's going to be taking action. It's going to be looking to beat these in my going. She'll be looking to win in these environments. And here we've got an agent. The agent is our artificial intelligence. That's the person or that's the mind that's going to be navigating these environments and learning from the feedback that their minds are going to be giving it in order to perform certain actions. And so the way it works is the agent performs certain actions in this environment. And as a result the state in which it is in will change so it might be further or closer or more to the left more to the right. It might have sort of the other parameters that describe its state and those parameters. So the state is going to change because of the action taken and it will also get rewards based on the action. So every time it takes an action the state will change and it'll

13

get rewarded. Now bear in mind sometimes it might happen that it won't change the state, the action won't change a stay or there won't be a reward for taking that action. In that sense it was. But nevertheless the agent's going to keep doing that was going to be taking actions cheating the state getting rewards changing action taking actions changing the state and getting rewards. And by doing that process it's going to be learning about what was going to be exploring the environment, understanding what actions lead to good rewards and favorable states and what actions the two rewards an unfavorable state. And this is a very simplistic representational very global problem. So if you think about it, environments actually don't have to be just mazes. It's not just about getting out of a maze or finding a treasure in a maze. An environment can be pretty much anything in life. So imagine you waking up in the morning and cooking an omelet. So in order to make that omelet you need to go through certain steps. You need to get the salt, get the eggs, get the frying pans which to fire on and so on and it does sound like a routine mundane thing. But it's become routine because you've done it so many times. But in reality it's an environment where you're performing certain actions you're taking that you put the fire on you putting a frying pan on the fire you're putting all the eggs into the frying pan and you put some salt on the eggs and you're turning over and so on. So as you can see they are CRN actions which are taken in certain states and those actions lead to certain other states and sometimes reward. So for instance when you put the fire on and you wait wait wait wait wait you take an action of wait wait wait wait too long and then you put the eggs into the frying pan. The rewards are going to be very negative. It's all going to burn. On the other hand if you do all the all the correct actions in the correct time so it's also very important to understand that actions should be taken at the correct points in time. So for instance putting the salt in the frying pan before you put the eggs in might not be the best idea. You might want to take that action of putting the salt into the frying pan after the eggs are in there so that they are in a different state. So it's important to remember that. And at the same time so if you take all the correct actions in the correct order in the correct states your final reward could be that you get an omelet which you can eat. And so that's a very basic activity in your life but if you think about it it is actually an environment and you are the agent going through this environment and performing a task you don't really need to learn anything because you already know it pretty well. But at the same time you could learn, maybe you could learn how to make a better omelet or especially if it's your first omelet that you're making you're probably going to screw it up. But you will learn from that because you will understand what actions lead towards states and routes and anything else in life. For instance even trading on the stock market and you know buying and selling and getting certain feedback from the market in the sense of returning positive or negative returns. That's also an environment that's you participating in that environment as an aged.

What Is Reinforcement Learning?

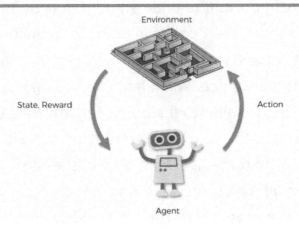

Driving a car is also an environment where you can turn the steering wheel, you can accelerate, you can break and so on and you're getting feedback from the environment and you know one of those feedbacks is the policeman giving you a speeding fine if you're going above the acceptable or allowed speed limit on that highway. And therefore from there you learn that that's not something that should be done because it leads to a negative reward. So rewards don't have to be just at the very end of the process. They can be throughout the journey throughout the process. So those are a couple of examples. And in terms of a I the simplest way to think of reinforcement learning is like training a dog when you train the dog you to give it certain commands and if it obeys those commands then you give it a reach you give it like a biscuit or something if it doesn't Abeles Kamaz you tell it that it's a bad dog or you just don't give it a treat. And through that process it learns what certain commands or what it needs to do, what action it needs to take in certain states and the states are the commands that you're giving it. And based on that it will get some certain rewards of course in the world of AI. It's not that complex. You don't have to give the treats. You don't have to have a bag of biscuits with you every time you just give it a plus one or a minus one so it's a huge advantage that in the world of AI we've created these AIs ourselves. So the rewards that we're giving them if you think wow these are really cool rewards are giving them they don't actually exist they're just a plus or minus one or plus a one or a zero or something. So it's all nonexistent, all imaginary stuff. But at the same time it leads to great results as we can create these amazing things, these amazing artificial intelligence as by this amazing artificial intelligence by just providing rewards we don't really exist. Plus and minus one doesn't cost anything but at the same time release results. So it is very similar to the real world. And you know for example Dokes But here the rewards are digital and just numbers.

What Is Reinforcement Learning?

And with that in mind we can talk about robot dogs. I love this example so this is just around in pictures not necessarily that exact robot dog you know that is trained through reinforcement learning some of the robot dogs especially the older ones you'd have an algorithm in there. And this is actually a good example of the difference between pre-programmed agents and reinforcement learning agents, so you could have a robot dog which is preprogrammed to how to walk. So in the in the algorithm behind the dog in the software will say OK so in order to walk you need to move your left leg forward left front leg forward then your back right leg forward then your front right leg forward then your back left leg forward and repeat that action and you know that's that's the definition of walking is a function inside this dog. And then it might have you know how to sit, how to stand and things like that. Whereas in a robot dog that is trained through reinforcement learning what happens is you don't pre program it. This is the key concept to everything here that you don't have any algorithm inside that is hard coded into the dog. Instead you have what we'll be discussing in the future. You have this reinforcement learning algorithm which is told that is OK so the goal is to get from where you are now not knowing anything to that to the end of the room for example. And here are the certain actions you can take. You can move your right foot you can move your left foot you can move your right back foot you are left back foot so here all the degrees of freedom you can do you can move it like this you can move like that so like a list of actions you can take and your rewards are every time you take a step forward you get a plus one every time you fall over. You get a minus one and that's all there is to it.

What Is Reinforcement Learning?

And then they just leave the dog and let it figure it out on its own. So the dog tries to stand up and it falls , then it realizes that OK I shouldn't do that action that led to me falling because every time I fall I get a minus one which is not good for me then. So does the other action that helps him stand up and then it figures are just experiments, experiments , experiments tri's things randomly and then figures out that it can make a step forward by moving its right front foot and he gets a plus one and realizes oh I should do more of that. OK cool so it now learns that it should do more of this and less of that. And through this learning process it quickly very quickly understands how it can walk. And those dogs that figured out on their own can actually sometimes walk better than dogs that are pre programmed because of really preprogrammed things. We look at real life dogs and or you know we use our own imagination to do it whereas a reinforcement learning dog can optimize things on its own. And because in AI sometimes it can get even better results. And that's how they can train these robots. The same robot dogs play soccer. You can train a normal dog to play soccer because you know simply the whole approach is different. And it's not something that you know probably a normal dog has been trained to do or has ever done in its process of its evolution. Whereas a reinforcement learning robot dog can very easily understand how to play soccer as long as you tell them what the rewards are, what the goals are and the possible actions they can take. So that is how reinforcement learning works. In general there's a quick overview of reinforcement learning. I hope that got you very excited about what was going to come next because it's a completely different world compared to preprogram solutions, hard program hardcoded solutions where you have the if-else conditions. This is very different. And we're going to be talking more about that. In the meantime we've got some additional reading for you so if you'd like to have some supporting materials Here's a great article which you can look at and look into. It's called simple reinforcement learning with tensor flow. It's got ten parts. The link is here and you'll find the full clickable link on. In the course of resources by Arthur Giuliani's 2016 article, you can follow along this course and also get additional information from that article. But bear in mind that that article tends to flow whereas in this course we are using pi torche so different implementations but implantations but at the same time you might pick up a few things here and there that might supplement your learning that we're going to be doing in this course. So great articles follow you in if you're considering following it for sure. Still just in case. Check out that first part and see if you like it, see if you'd like to read it a bit more.

Additional Reading

Additional Reading:

Simple Reinforcement Learning with Tensorflow (10 Parts)

By Arthur Juliani (2016)

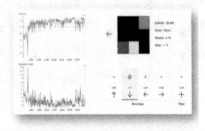

Link:

https://medium.com/emergent-future/simple-reinforcement-learning-with-tensorflow-part-0-q-learning-with-tables-and-neural-networks-d195264329d0

And then we've got specific to this project, border enforcement learning. There's a paper by Richard Sutton which is called reinforcement learning. One introduction is that the 1998 papers are quite old but at the same time you can learn a bit about reinforcement learning, some of the examples like that omlet example and other examples of where reinforcement learning can be applied and just a general overview of reinforcement learning. If you are looking for some additional reading and on that note we're going to wrap up this project. Can't wait to see you next time.

THE BELLMAN EQUATION

Today we're going to talk about the Bellman equation. It's quite a complex topic and we're going to introduce it in a step by step manner throughout this whole section of the course so I'm not going to just jump straight into the most complex version of the Belmont equation right away but instead we're going to introduce it slowly in order to gradually understand how it works. And I hope your goal with that approach if you're G.R. Let's get straight into it. So we're going to have a couple of key concepts that we're going to be operating with and these concepts are. S stands for states so the state in which our agent is or any other possible state in which it can be represents an action that an agent can take. So an agent can have access to a certain list of actions and actions are very important when they're looked at in a state combination. So when you're in a swing state and then you look at actions and it starts to make sense what's going to be the result of those actions because you'll look an action by itself or a state doesn't really make sense because you don't know where you are and where you can possibly end up and then we have we'll have our Which stands for reward and that's through ward that agent gets for entering into a certain state and gamma is the discount factor. And we'll talk about the discount factor in a second all make sense just now but they're just taking notes. Make a mental note that we are going to have this letter Gamelin that will be operating with later on. So the person behind the bellman equation is Richard Ernest bellman. He was a flight mathematician and came up with the concepts of dynamic programming which we now call reinforcement learning or which we call the Bellman equation now. Well that's what we're called now. And in 1953 he came up with that concept and that's when the Belmont Bellman equation came to me. So let's have a look at how this all works. There's our lovely agent in the bottom left corner and he is in a maze and this is quite a classical maze where you've got some blocks the wide blocks are blocks in which the agent can step into the gray block is the one one that is just not accessible says like a wall in this maze. The green is where the agent should be aiming to end up. That's where we want the agent to go. That's the finish. And the red is fire pits or the engine falls into the fire pit. He will lose the game. So in the fire pit the reward which is R is minus 1. So that's our way of telling the agent that's not something we want you to do. Like remember in the example of when we're training dogs we want to tell them like bad dog if it's not doing the right thing that wanted to do same thing here we're one tell the agent that this is not something that you should be doing you shouldn't be ending up in the square so every time it doesn't happen the squirrel get a minus one reward so you'll be punished with minus one reward. On the other hand if it ends up in the Green Square it will get a plus one reward meaning that that is what we wanted to do. So those are the two rewards that the agent can't possibly get. And how does it learn how to operate in this maze? Just like in that example of the robot dogs that learned to walk which is going to let it know it will just tell it that here is the action you can do. You can go up right, left or down. Those are four possible actions that you can take and that's it. Have a play around with that and see what you can come up with. So the agent might go to the right then they might go two more to the right they might go back to the left just randomly pressing the button and they're trying to see what happens and they go back here. They go up go up go down go up go right. So for now they haven't learnt anything, they just so far nothing's happened. They go right and then bam they end up in the Green Square. So they realize wow I just got a plus one awar So as soon as I stepped into the Green Square they got a plus one reward. And that triggers the algorithm to say OK that's really cool.

The Bellman Equation

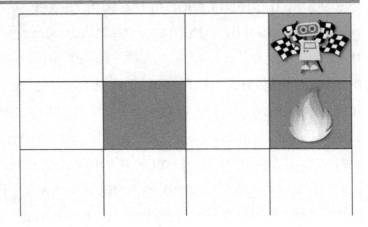

I am rewarded for ending up in the square so I want to end up in the square. So what does that mean for the agent? That means it starts to ask the question how did I get to this square. What was the preceding state I was in and what action that I took to get to square and then look back and say OK so the preceding state was this one. It turns out to be valuable in that state. The one that sparked the Red Arrow. Because from that state you're I'm I'm just one step away from getting the maximum reward I can possibly dream of plus one like a biscuit for a dog from as soon as I know if I ever am in that state. That square is marked with the Red Arrow. All I have to do is press right. So how do I tell myself to remember that that state is valuable. Well to me there's no difference actually as the agent. There's no difference in whether I am in the Green Square or in the white square right in the Green

Square I get the reward of one. So I'm going to mark for myself that the Y Square is got for me it has a value of 1 because it leads exactly to reward one. As soon as I'm in the white square I know I'll just take one more action. I'll be in the Green Square and I'll get a reward or one so that's why I'm going to say that the value of this square is equal to one because it leads directly to if on any sort of subtractions as soon as I mean here I know my reward will be one so I'm going to mark this square as the call to one that's the value that's the perceived value of being in the state. Next the agent's going to be OK. So how do I get into this square? And you know he might walk around again and so on. And up in the square again and be like OK how did I get into this square before that. And the way I got into this square was from this square. Interesting. OK so as soon as I get into this square I know that all I have to do is go right. And then from here I already know that I'm going to win. I know exactly how everything is going to unravel from here and I know the value of being in this state is equal to one. And since there's no nothing stopping me from growing from here to here the value in this is going to a perceived value. I'm great value being in here as a vehicle to want as well because this is what I mean here I know. Be here and I'll be here pretty quickly. So I'm going to win. And then how do you get into this square before that. Well I got into this square from this square. So the value is a similar approach. The value of being here is also equal to one and so on so the value of being here is equal to one value of being here is equal to one because each one of them leads to the next one and these to the finish line. So that's all pretty logical at this stage. This is us pretty much designing the Bellman equation right now. So this is we could possibly think about designing an equation that helps an agent go through the maze. So look at the reward then the preceding state give it a value of equal to reward the proceedings and so those are kind of like creates a pathway is all great and well but the problem here is OK what happens if our agent for some reason starts in this state instead of starting here and taking these actions and that it actually starts in the state. How does it know how it remembers which action to take should it go right or should it go down or should maybe go left or should go up. How does it remember which is the next continuation from here? If the only values it has are these values are equal to once it kind of cannot see what's further away. It can only see. All right. What I have here and what I have here. How does it know which way to go? Well at this stage it doesn't it's as pretty identical for the age and which way to go. And so that's why this approach doesn't really work. It's a very simplistic explanation. Of course there's much more to it. But in an intuitive way that's why we cannot just assign just carry on this value backwards like that. Because one of the reasons is once Agent is in between these two values which is where it is going to go. It doesn't get confused like that. And so how do we solve this problem? What are we going to do? And this is where we're going to start introducing the Bellman equation in its actual form slowly step by step. So the Bellman equation looks something like this. So we've already talked about the value of being in a certain state as is your current state or any given state and there is as well. And as Prime is the state the following state the state that you will end up in after the state and by taking concerted action. But we know that there's many actions an agent can take and that's why we've got this Max over here. So by taking an action what will happen to an agent so let's say we're in state as by taking an action in state assets and we take action. What will happen is you will instantly get a reward by getting into a new state. And remember that reward can be one or plus one or minus one if it's at the end of the game or it can be a zero if it's throughout the game in this case our reward throughout the game is zero. So that's the reward Plus we will get into a new state which has the value of s prime. So that's the value of the new state and gamma. We'll talk about it in a second. But the point I'm trying to raise here or the point I'm raising here is that you've got many different actions that we can take and that's why we've got the maximum. So by taking action we get reward Plus we end up in a new state. And so for every move out of the in our case before our possible actions for every one of the possible 4 actions we're going to have an equation like this. So this is going to have a value for they will have a different value for every one of four actions and we're going to look at only the maximum because of course the agent wants to take the optimal state. So if he's in state s he's going to look at these values he's going to find the maximum based on the action and going to take that action that needs the maximum of these values. So hopefully that makes sense why we're taking the maximum here. Then once we got the reward and the value that said why do we have this Gabaa parameter here. Well it's there exactly to solve that problem of where the agent doesn't know which way to go because it cannot. It's comparing the values of two states on both sides and they're the same.

The Bellman Equation

$$V(s) = \max_a(R(s, a) + \gamma V(s'))$$

That's why the gamblers called the discounting factor so we're going to have a look at that and it better understand. So let's take a formula I'll put it here on the top right. And now we will analyze what the values of the different states are. And every state here is a square. No. So one of these white squares is a state. I mean we're going to calculate the value of being in that state. So let's start with the square. What is the value of being in this state? Well we need to take the maximum of this value across all actions. And we know that this value is maximized as we get closer to the finish line and that's how it is constructed and by just looking at it you can see because here's got the reward and here's got a discounting factor multiplied by the value of the next state. And it just makes sense that that's how we would construct that equation so it makes sense that from here the maximum of this value will be if we move to the right. So that's how we calculate the values that this value of this state is he calls the maximum or equals to this value. If we move to the right if we take an action of moving to the right. So what will this value be? Well the reward of moving to the right is equal to 1. And regardless what color gamma is we don't have a value in the state because we are already in the best state possible. So this is the final stage. It won't have a value, we just get a reward here and that's the end of the game. So the value of this maximum will be equal to 1. And that's why the value of the state here is equal to 1. Now things get interesting when we move to the left when we move backwards a bit. So now is to calculate the value of being in this state and for that we're going to need Gabaa. So let's say our discounting factor is a zero point nine and it makes sense what a discounting factor is once we calculate that. So from here just based on our intuition and based because we know how this is working how this works. We know that the best possible action is to go to the right because from here we go here. So that means the maximum will be achieved in this state if you go to the right. And so let's see what happens if we plug it in here. So if you go from here to here you don't get in, your reward will be zero. But then you'll get camis who get zero point nine times the value of the new state which is one. So in this case the value of the whole result of this is 1 times a 0.9 times one equals 2.9. So that's all values per. So if we calculate this now you'll see that from here. We know just by looking at the maze we know because we are humans because we're understanding how this equation works. Of course an AI agent would have to experiment with these things. But because we have like a crystal ball we can see this whole maze. We have a bird's eye view right now. We know that the best action is to go to the right. So if we plug it all in here it'll be zero no reward Plus the report nine times the value in the state 0.9 is zero point eighty one and so on. So here it'll be 0.23 and he'll be 0.66. So you can see that the way the discounted factor works is it discounts the value of the state as you are further away.

So if you are familiar with finance theory then it's something similar to time value of money like what would you think about it this way What would you prefer to have $5 today or $5 in 10 days from now. Just if somebody was to give you a choice I will give you five dollars today all you $5 10 days from all. Of course you would choose $5 today. Why is that? Well because you can take that $5 and you can invest them at a certain interest rate which is very similar to gamma. And your $5 in 10 days will actually grow into maybe 5 dollars and 73 cents or something like that. And that's how the time value of money works. And a very similar concept here. And the important thing to understand here is that this is just a theory, a way of reinforcement learning. So Richard Belman came up with this equation. And from then on, that's how we use it. So you could go ahead and come up with a different equation. It doesn't have to have Gamla, it might have some other factor that you know has a factor. But this approach works and that's why we're using and this is what it looks like so the further away you are the less value of it being in the state and in terms of time and money. If I could say to you where you would rather be, would you rather be here? Would you rather be here? You'd say I would rather be here. So we're creating that same phenomenon as time value of money we're artificially creating it through gamma so that in order to incentivize agents or inspire agents to be closer to the finish line.

The Bellman Equation

$$V(s) = \max_{a}(R(s, a) + \gamma V(s'))$$

V=0.81	V=0.9	V=1	
V=0.73			
V=0.66			

$\gamma = 0.9$

So if an agent were to be asked would you rather be here or here because of the way this equation works it would choose to be here. There's nothing more to that, nothing less. It's not something that the world works this way. No it's just something that we're artificially creating in order for our agents to understand that this is good this is good this is good old good but this one is better than this one and this one is better than this one and this one has been in this one. And that way you can see all the agents can see in which direction they need to go. So it can see that if I'm standing here remember that problem that we had or was he standing here so if you are standing here do I go down or if I'm suddenly here to go up or do I go down. Well now there's not a problem anymore because he can see that it's actually better to go up because the values are here. And then from here he's got to go right because the value is bigger here than here. And then from here Bertschi goes right because the value here is bigger than you know. And from here he already knows that he needs to go right because he'll get a reward here. So that's how this whole approach works. Now let's have a quick look at the rest of the square. So how do we calculate the value in this square? Well here is where things get tricky. So from here you might not actually go left right you might actually go right so we can just keep going like that because it might actually be shorter to go this way. So what we're going to do is we're going to calculate the value in the square first. And because obviously from here the best way to go is up. Again that's because we see the crew, we have the crystal ball, we can see things and you'll see further down in the section you'll see how the agent actually explores this and understands this on their own terms through experimentation. But for us we know that it's better to go this way so we're going to calculate value here and that's why we're going to calculate the value in this square first. So here we have three possible actions. In reality we actually have four we can also go left. The agent could hypothetically press left and bump into the wall and stay here. But for simplicity, a set which is going to show the actions that we know and having the crystal ball we know which actions are the ones actually lead to something other than the same state again. And so here from here we know that again just because we have a crystal ball we know that the best way to go is this way an agent of course would have to experiment and find the best way and you'll see how that happens. Further down in the section you'll see actually how an agent walks around and how you would experiment trying to find these values. But for us we know it's that way. So here if we plug everything in one so the maximum the best output is when you go up. And here is a report 9:0 So you put that in. You get zero point nine. OK so it is Kalika that calculates this one. Same approach. There are three ways you can go. Actually four for the agent but for us we can see it's only three. So zero point eighty one from here you have ZERO point seventy three. And it actually ties in nicely with this value because if you discount again you put 66 and here you have 0.23 because this is the optimal route.

The Bellman Equation $V(s) = \max_{a}(R(s,a) + \gamma V(s'))$

$\gamma = 0.9$

V=0.81	V=0.9	V=1	
V=0.73		V=0.9	
V=0.66	V=0.73	V=0.81	V=0.73

So there you go. That is the value of all of these states. And now you can see that because we've created this equation or we've created synthetically this whole concept of the closer you are to the finish line the more valuable that state is not because we're afraid that now it's pretty obvious for the agent which way it should go. And we'll talk more about that in the coming. I hope you enjoyed today's session and I know it's a bit. It might sound a bit very basic at this stage but as we go through this section we will add a bit more complexity to it. At the same time if you cannot wait if you want to jump into it then there is a paper which you can look at and it is the original paper by Richard Belman. It's called the theory of dynamic programming from 1954. And you can find it at this link. And there you go so you can jump straight into it and read from the author of the Bellman equation. But just bear in mind that this is quite a mathematically heavy paper. And on that note I'll look for your next.

THE PLAN

So we've talked about the Bellman equation and we've analyzed our little maze. Let's have a look at the plan. What is the plan? Well here is our main analysis. And we know that we can actually see the values of each state. We can see what the value of being in every single state is. Therefore the AI can or the agent can navigate this maze. So what is the plan? Well the plan is simply like a treasure map for artificial intelligence instead of looking at these values that just replace them with arrows which indicate in which direction the agent should go. Because of those because it knows those values. So an ideal scenario after it's explored this environment. It knows the value of being in each state and therefore you can come up with this map. So let's have a look again.

The Bellman Equation

V=0.81	V=0.9	V=1	
V=0.73		V=0.9	
V=0.66	V=0.73	V=0.81	V=0.73

We know that your values are one so if you are here out of the two the better one is this Once you go right from here out of the two this one is a better one this one is a better one. This one is a better one. Or actually from here you have two options right. So he was kind of like a tie so just picking one at random doesn't matter which one because the value in these in either case is the same and more so even if you look through it will take the same amount of steps and the same number of steps to get to the end. From here you've got three options but this one is the better value from here. This one is a better value from here. Obviously this was a better value because you know you just get it minus one reward right away. And from here you have like three actually but this one is the best one of the best values of the state. And so therefore if we replace them with arrows it makes sense that this is how the agent would go if it starts here or for some reason it ends up in this square. It knows how to get out of here. Stars and this square know how to get on here and so on. So that is what a plan is. And don't confuse plan with policy because we're going to be talking about policies for Iran that are very similar to plans but they have a little trick to them because the environment's going to be a bit different. It's going to be stochastic and that's what we're going to talk about in the next project.

MARKOV DECISION PROCESS

And today we're talking about Mark of decision processes or M.D.. Let's have a look at what we've got today. So last time we stopped on the concept of a map. So because we've calculated the values based on the Bellman equation we can derive this map for our agent on this maze. And basically what that means is wherever the angle an agent starts let's say it starts over there. It knows exactly which steps to take in order to get to the finish line so it just goes up right. Right and done. And so the question here is is that it. Is it really that simple? Is reinforcement learning really that you know for the lack of a better word boring. It's yeah. Once you have the math that's it all you have to do is you've done it just full of them. Well the reality is that it's not actually that simple. And that's a good thing because it makes this course more interesting for us and we can actually solve much more complex problems. So this is where a mark of a process is coming. But first we're going to talk about two things. We're into it deterministic search versus non-deterministic search. So let's talk about the concept of deterministic search. This is our agent in the maze and deterministic search means that if the agent decides to go up then what will happen is 100 percent probability it will go up. That's exactly what will happen. There's no other option. Once it says go up or click the up arrow it'll go up. There's no other option. Now on the other hand non deterministic search is when our agent says it wants to go up. There are actually a couple of options. For example there could be three options and we're going to look an example where there are three options but it doesn't have to be a limit to three before it could be different depending on depends on the problem the randomness could be different but in our case it could be three options with an 80 percent chance he does go up. But then with a 10 percent chance when he wants to go up he'll actually go to the left just because. Because that's how the environment works, that's the world that he lives in. And with another check in 10 percent chance he'll actually go right. And in this case he'll fall into the firepit. So that is how it all works. That's an example of a nondeterministic sure search a stochastic process and what the point of this is is to make a more realistic model of what could actually happen in a real world in a real world type of problem because very rarely do you get situations like this when you do something and it happens exactly that way. And even if you think about it in terms of games let's say you've got an agent playing Pac-Man. Well not always is it the case that if he's standing in the square he goes up. He will get the same exact result every time. Well he will indeed go up but it may be in one case you won't get eaten by a ghost in either case. He will get eaten by a ghost. So as you can see there's some randomness to it because it depends on how the ghosts are moving and they don't always move the same way.

Markov Decision Process (MDP)

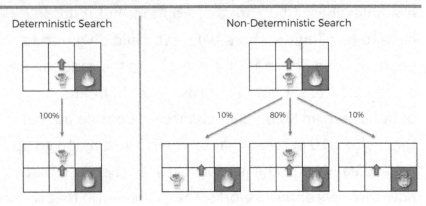

They don't always start in the same locations. So it's very logical is very fair that there is some randomness there's something that is not under the control of the agent and that is this is just a way for us to present that in order for us to learn how we can deal with it and how that affects a Bellman equation how it affects the whole reinforcement learning process. But at the same time the randomness is of course not limited to if you go up there's a 10 percent chance you'll go right or temp's and just go left or if you go down to 10 percent chance you go right or left or you're right there's a 10 percent chance an up or down subtle limited to where you're going to end up sometimes you might have a problem that is exactly. Sometimes the possibilities might be different. Sometimes the randomness might boil down to something else; it might be boiled down like that example. Pacman ghosts eating you are not eating you or it might boil down to something different. For instance like if the agent is playing Doom and then there's something like a monster which is going to shoot him in one case and in other cases there's like there's a probability if we all get shot and we won't get shot. And so and so something that is out of the control of the agents is something I cannot predict. That's what we are modeling here in nondeterministic search and this is where we have directly approached two new concepts: a mark of processes and or a mark of process and a marker mark of decision process so let's have a look at these. And you know how much I don't like to put definitions and lots of text on the side. But in this case it is necessary for us to go through that. So let's have a look at a stochastic process that has a mark of property. If the conditional probability distribution of future states of the process conditional and both past and present state depends only upon the present state not on the sequence of events that preceded it. A process with this property is called a marker. Very complex definition and it kind of like you introduce a little bit not only contradicts itself but feels like it contradicts itself so here it is conditional for positive presence that depends on your point. But at the same time it only depends upon the present state. So don't get too bogged down in that. I'll break it down in simple terms so a mark of property is when your future states. So not just your choice but the whole thing. Your choice and the environment it will only like the results of all of the action you take in that environment will only depend on where you are now. It will not depend on how you got there. And that's it. So that's a matter of public and a process which has this property is called the market process. So to put it into an example so if your agent is here and if he goes if he decides to go up he might go. In our case in our non deterministic search example he actually might go left and right. All right. That's because we have that stick in this city inside our environment. We have that randomness inside our environment. So any one of these things might happen. But the key here is that this is a mark of progress because we don't care how you got here. He could have come from the top and ended up here he could have come from the left and that up here you could come from the bottom and end up here. He could have played a move around here like 100000 times and then got here. It does not matter what happened before, only what matters is which state he is in now. And so the probabilities of going left or right or up will always be the same if he's in this state now. And so that's basically just saying it doesn't matter what happened before we're here now. This is the state you're in. And don't forget that state doesn't just mean where he's standing. The state is the state of the whole of the agent in the environment so there are monsters on the right or the monsters on the left or you know is the ghost coming from the top or bottom whatever state you're in now.

Doesn't matter how you got there doesn't matter how and how it all came to be that you're there in that state. Now what will happen in the future is only determined by the state you're in now. Plus the actions you will take them plus of course the randomness that is overlaid on top of that. So that's a mark of process and a marker decision process or an MVP or marker decision process. Provide a mathematical framework for modeling decision making in situations where outcomes are partly random and partly under control over decision making. So important to understand that the mark of decision process processes are different and different from the whole concept mark of process to mark of process. They are like a mathematical framework. But at the same time I thought it was important for us to understand what a mark of a process is because I think it still helps in understanding the mark of the decision process and so a mark of the decision process is there. This is exactly what we've been discussing Up till now so that the agent lives in this environment where he has control like him previously and had full control of what's going on but now it has a little bit less control. It can decide to go up but it actually knows. OK so if I go up there's an apes chance I'll go up this attempt and chances go left and chance will go right. So not everything is fully under its control. There is some randomness in this environment and that's exactly what a mark of decision process and Markov decision process is the framework that the agent will use in order to understand what to do in this environment. So we've got an environment with some toxicity and some randomness. And now the agent has to choose for instance should go up down left or right. He has to make that decision. He doesn't know what to do. And in order to make that decision is going to apply a framework is going to be using a mark of decision process in order to make that decision what what's going to happen where it's going to go. And so basically this environment that poses this problem is referred to as the mark of decision process so it's the framework the agent uses at the same time the environment is referred to that the agent is operating in a market decision process environment. And so basically here we have two concepts. We've got the mark of the process is the way this environment is designed that the PA does the work. What happens from where you are now doesn't depend on the past. And that same time we've got the mark of the decision process is the framework that the agent is going to be using in order to solve this environment.

Markov Decision Process (MDP)

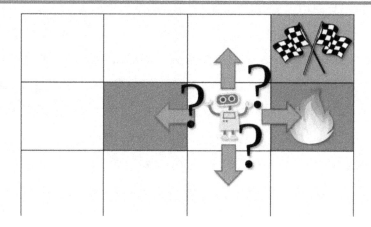

And the good news is that the mark of the decision process or that framework that we're talking about is actually just an add-on to our Bellman equation question. It is the Bellman equation but just a bit more sophisticated. So let's have a look at that. This is our Bellman equation so far. It's the maximum of all possible actions. So the value of being in a state is the maximum of all possible actions that you can take from that state. The maximum is taken from the reward that you would get by taking that action in that state plus a discount factor times the value of the next state which is as prime. So that's what we've had so far. Now because we have some randomness in our whole process this this part will change because we don't actually know which state will end up and we don't know what s prime will be will it be if we're going up will it be up or will be left will be right so we actually have to place this with the expected value of the next date. So here we're going to replace this so there's three possible states we can end up in. And so we're going to replace that with some value that state has a value of as one prime. That it has a view of as prime to prime. And this state has a value of the three Bryne. So now we're going to multiply the state that we actually are intending to go into by 80 percent because that's how probability of getting to that state plus the probability of getting to this state is 10 percent plus people getting in-state So this is just our expected value so if from statistics if we take the expected value of getting into the state that we'll get into these are kind of like the average What's the average of what we'll get and then we replace that over here. Then we get this aggression and it jumps very quickly just because it's big but if you look at it carefully you'll see the same thing said about Max here Max here. Then you've got r of S and A R of S and there you've got gamma you've got gamma. And then finally here you've got v. So you knew exactly it was a deterministic search and you knew which states you'll get into. Now you don't know which state you'll get into since that of taking V. You're taking the expected value of the state you'll get into or of the future state or just in simpler terms you're just taking the average of what you will be getting into.

Markov Decision Process (MDP)

$$0.8 * V(s'_1) + 0.1 * V(s'_2) + 0.1 * V(s'_3)$$

$$V(s) = \max_a (R(s, a) + \gamma V(s'))$$

So you know like it was like for 30 plus 3 percent chance it will be like this Plus's divide by three basically. But in this case it's not, it's not exactly like average. It's a weighted average because of the probabilities here. So here you've got the probability of it when you're in this stage to take this action of getting into state as prime time the value of s prime and some to cross all these primes that you could possibly get into who we are. So exactly what we had three here one two three. Add them up, multiply them, add them up. Same here. One two three. Multiply them by the probabilities and add them up. And that is your new Bellman equation. Congratulations. This is what we're going to be working with going forward. And that is the framework that is used in decision processes so that is the framework that solves this. Those agents used to solve this whole stochastic non deterministic search problem where there's random events that are happening that they cannot control. So it's much more complex. But as you can see because we've built up slowly to it. Now we already know about this we know about. There's worry about this. We know about this. We know what they are. So all we did is we just introduced this part over here because there are probabilities involved in the action or the consequences of your action on nondeterministic they are based on probabilities. And so there we go. That's how a marker of decision process works and the underlying equation behind it.

Markov Decision Process (MDP)

$$V(s) = \max_a \left(R(s, a) + \gamma \sum_{s'} P(s, a, s') V(s') \right)$$

Once again it is something that more closely resembles real world problems real or Sinatras or even game scenarios because not everything is straightforward.

There is some randomness of all involved and not always will taking an action in a certain state will always Nawal not always will lead to the same outcome. And so this is what we're going to be dealing with going forward and that's going to make things way more interesting. So hopefully you're excited for that and excited to see what's going to come next. And in the meantime I found a really cool paper for you to have a look at this time. It's a very applied paper. So this one is actually really interesting to read through. It's called a survey of applications of Mark of decision processes process and it was written by white in 1993. Here's the link and I'll show you examples of where Markov decision processes actually are used to model real life Sinatras. I think I was very excited by this. I was impressed by some examples of population harvesting for instance. So let's say you have some fish and you know what the population of fish is. You need to decide how many fish we can fish out this year and what. So that's your current state. That's the action that you're taking. How many can we shoot this year? So what are the possible outcomes of that? How many fish will we have next year? How many fish will we have the year after and the year after and so on. And it's not deterministic because it's not like if you take it at an hour and 90 percent of the population the next year you will have you know back to 100 percent is not not exactly sermonizing. There are certain random factors involved which are out of our control and therefore we have to understand what's going to happen. We have to model what's going to happen. That's where a market decision processes agriculture. There's an example like something like harvesting crops: how much crops do we harvest, how much money do we not harvest. Another one which I looked at finance and investment like an insurance company needs to decide how much of its funds it will invest in any I think day or year or some period of time and there are those certain factors that are out of his control. For instance you know the market movements, it doesn't know what can happen so it needs to actually model that somehow. A mark of decision processes used for that. So here you can see lots and lots of examples. And this is the number of examples given I think for each one. And so you know even sports examples for sports and epidemics and motor insurance claims inspections and maintenance and repairs it's also very interesting. Have a look at that. Just to give you an understanding of hey this is not just all made up stuff hypothetical The Matrix type of thing. This is actually the real world scenario so I'll give you a better understanding and this is what we talked about in the promotional video for the scores or the description of the course that we're going to inspire you and your intuition to give you ideas for how to use AI in real life. This is your opportunity. Look at this paper to understand. OK so we're going to be dealing with the mark of the decision process going forward. It's really cool what they look like in real life and this could possibly trigger some ideas for you on how you could apply in the future to make the world a better place and we'd be super happy about that. We'd be happy if you could use what you learn in this course to make the world a better place.

POLICY VS PLAN

Previously we had quite a strenuous and long project on Margrove decision processes and hopefully you got along well with that. And hopefully I could explain things in an approachable and engaging way. And today we're going to talk about policies versus plans. There will be a quick and fun project because now we're entering into a new world we're entering into a world of stochastic search non deterministic search when you're just not getting through the maze but also accounting for random factors that might just hit you in the head when you're going through this maze and you need to be prepared for it. That's the world. Our agent is living in and it's more fun but it's also more dangerous it's more it's less predictable. So how is our agent going to behave? Let's have a look. There's our mark of decision process framework which is once again our favor Bellman equation. However the more advanced version of the Bellman equation we are working with. So from now on we're just going to call this the Beldon equation. And here we've got our maximal and Crucell action so the value of a state, any state, is the maximum across all actions an agent could possibly perform in that state. And the maxim was taken from the reward that the agent will get by performing action A instate as Plus a discount factor multiplied by the expected value of the new state it will be in. And I'd expect those taken here because they don't know exactly what saddle they end up in. There are some random effects that are present in the environment that might alter the state and might not end up in the desired state. It might end up in a different state. That's why we're taking the expected value over here somewhere here. So let's have a look at this as our example or in our example of the maze. So this is what we had previously so previously we're dealing with live deterministic search. So we knew that. All right so if I'm here I definitely need to go here if I'm here. I definitely need to go here if I'm here I definitely need to go here if I'm here I'm here. So it was all pretty straightforward. Once you have this map and remember to call it, we called it a plan. Once you have the plan it's pretty straightforward to do.

Policy vs Plan

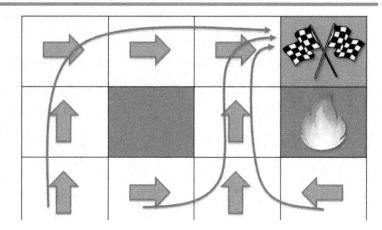

There are. So that's the plan with arrows. And from here it was very straightforward we're this is these are the routes that they will take whenever you start on this blue line. That's exactly the way you'd go. However, now we don't have a plan anymore. We can't have a plan because you know whatever we plan might not happen it's not under control or plan is when you know exactly what you need to do next. You know the steps. So you have a starting point, you have a goal and you know every single step so you can plan them out like I'll do this one I'll do this one I'll do this like in life like a plan. But at the same time there's so much randomness going on. You can have a plan because what if you get here and then you click to the right and actually take you down. So that's not part of your plan. So that's why it's called planning more. And here we're going to calculate the values and are actually going to just look at the calculated values for this same problem. But based on that given that we have this randomness inside. So these are the new values. And so why are these values different so let's just compare to what we had previously. This is what we had previously. These are then you. So once again we had previously because he won 3.9 percent. He was really 366. And this is what we have now aa less than once in force and 1 6 3. And by the way these are not exactly the current rallies off the top of my head but if we were to run an agent some values would be something similar to this and the values could change because depending on the gamble that it would choose 3.9 or other value but nevertheless for the for argument's sake these are the values that we're dealing with now and they're approximate they convey the whole notion in the correct way so let's have a look at them. Why have they changed? Well why is this one here the value was one. Why is it all of a sudden 0.26 Why is it less than one. Just go from here. Well we actually called because from here if we go right which is our intention if we go right we could I would actually we have a 10 percent chance we'd end up here. So we'd hit the wall and would be back in this state. And remember we have a Gamla So the value would be discounted and or we're off or off at 10 and chance would end up here in this state. So it's not a 100 percent probability I would get here so therefore the disvalue can no longer be a one, it's something less and it's 0.26. So that's an example of why it's like this. And you could get the exact value if you calculated the Bellman equation the full but my question that we have now. The only problem is that there's going to be some recursion because you would need to know the value for this and then you need to know the value for this. That is quite complex and that's why we're not doing the calculations manually here. That's why I can do them as I'm going through all this . It's like it's nothing too complex for me. You can't play these things. So that's our value here. But this is a different one. So here it is just 0.9 just because of the discounting factor. Remember from here to here again now from here we colleges jump from here to here simply because even if we jump if we go like this we might end up back here back here. Right this 20 percent chance that will still stay in the square because we'll hit a wall. And again and so on. So the value of being here is zero point seventy one. Again this and the discounting factor. You know this might look odd to you that this is even with the discount factor this is too high. Maybe the discounting factor in this example is not 0.9, maybe it's seven point ninety nine or something like that , so don't worry about that. Just kind of like focus on that. The values have indeed changed that the values are now less. Mostly because it's not a hundred percent probability to get to the state that you want to get and what you will find. An interesting one is here that here just to be 0.9 actually has dropped very much has dropped substantially. Why is that? Well because if you go from here up which is our intention there's a 10 percent chance of hitting a wall but there's a 10 percent chance of actually ending up in the firepit and losing minus one to reward and basically that means for the agent that's the end of the game. And so this is a very bad state to be in. So all of a sudden we remembered we had zero points nine years apart and so they were equivalent. Doesn't matter you hear here they're pretty much equal in terms of value of being in each of these states. But now all of a sudden bam this date is nearly twice as good as this one simply because here if you go straight to it you go right where you want to go. Then you know the consequences of the randomness occurring if you just stay here. Here one of the consequences is a 10 percent chance that you end up in the pit. So as you can see this is no longer such a good state anymore simply because of something that fluctuation that could happen.

Policy vs Plan

V=0.71	V=0.74	V=0.86	
V=0.63		V=0.39	
V=0.55	V=0.46	V=0.36	V=0.22

As you can see this one is also very bad because it's as bad as this one in terms of you know it's only 10 percent chance of ending up in the pit and 10 percent chance of ending up in the wall. But at the same time there's a discounting factor So first of all the discounting factor and also after this one you'd have to go here. And even if you hypothetically went here you could end up in the pit again. So that chance would also be taken into account because remember these values derive from this value and this value is derived from this value. Right. And therefore it's small but in reality actually what I said there was wrong. This value is not derived from the Fed. So if you just have a look now you will notice that this value over here is actually greater than this one. You will notice that for the agent it's better to go all this way than this way and it makes sense right. Because this way it doesn't lose it there's no chance of getting in the pit. Yes is a bit longer and therefore the discounting factor has a bigger effect. But at the same time simply because there's a chance of getting in the pit here if it goes straight it will there's a chance of jumping. So it will take a draw to take its time and just go around because that way there's a much lesser chance of it getting But there still is. So from here goes there it goes from here. It could potentially get into the pit because it could end up there and that could end up in the bill. But nevertheless it's a lesser chance so it will just go on like that. So very interesting to see how they're all changed. Remember previous you from here you'd go like that. From here you'd go like that and from here we go like that. And now all of a sudden you can see his change. Let's roll the arrows and see what it looks like now and voila. You see even a more random thing right. So yes this is true. But look at what happened here. Look at this one. Look at this one. Were you expecting that? That's something I definitely liked when I saw this one the first time I was very impressed. I was not super, I was not surprised and I was not expecting this at all. And this is an example of you know when I can outsmart a human. It sounds like something you caught even you could predict but the I through enforcement learning remember that example of dogs can actually sometimes work better than normal real life. Dogs are pre programmed robot dogs that can play soccer simply because they come up with these ideas that even we can't see. And as a great example you probably weren't expecting that as well that the Asians instead of going up is like why would I. Like if I go up then there's a 10 percent chance I'll jump into the pit. But what does it achieve by going into the war? Well 80 percent of the time will bump back and stay in the state. But 10 percent of the time will go here and 10 percent of the time I'll go here. So all of a sudden you can see that now it's actually in this new approach of jumping into the wall. There is a zero percent chance it will go into the fire but from this spot so. And it's like it really doesn't want to go into the fire pit so drugged bon bons into the wall a couple of times and then it will go the right or left at some point because that randomness is going to happen. And so it learned that through experimentation it learned that OK when I go forward the results are not as good as when I go to the wall. And if you think about it it's like this. This robot if you think about it this is a firepit is a very this is the this is like a square is like a very tiny ledge and then this is like a mountain like a cliff. And this robot is just hugging the cliff and just like trying to wait until it pushes right or left because well as a human you probably do the same you wouldn't be standing facing that way or you'd be hugging the cliff right. Or something like that. And hopefully you know we need to never end up in situations like that. But like visually just visually if you think about something here. And so that's pretty intense right. So that the AI came up with this idea and same here that is sort of going left and Riskin get in a fight but I'm just going to try balls off the wall like you know hug a wall try to jump into the wall and at some point I know that you know just there is a probability is a 10 percent chance every time I do that I'll go here and something will happen and I'll end up here and I'll be safe and then I'll just keep going like that. So a very very interesting approach that they took here and you can see that the routes are like this so from here it might go right and then it'll go right to the exit or here or go left like that. And here we will at some point you will go left and go like that again. This is important. I'm not a politician so even when it jumps from here it will go here. Maybe And then from here it might actually rain straight. It might actually go back to the right and then from here and I'm going to let me get that right. So there's lots of different options for it. Guys who might not follow this ironmonger go the other way. This is just the desired route that it's designed for itself. But the way it'll work out actually could be different. It depends on the real world. So there we go. That's the world of artificial intelligence. That's what a policy versus a plan is and hopefully you're slowly getting excited by what the AI can do especially given what we saw over here. These are some very virtuoso types of decisions that the AIs come up with. And as you can see when you're playing AI even from this small example you can see that even when you play in a real world maybe you'll come up with ideas and decisions that even sometimes humans can come up with. And that's exactly kind of like what happened in those games where the Google Alpha goal was played versus Lisa idole champion of goal in Korea back in the world championship of go. And they were playing in Korea back bakla in 2016 I think is March 2016. It came up with some moves that humans had never played in 3000 years or humans were not used to playing. And this is exactly an example of that. So once again hope you're getting excited and pumped about discourse and about what we can integrate.

ADDING A LIVING PENALTY

Today we're talking about the living penalty. Alright so here we've got all the Bellman equations and as we've been going through this course we've been slowly making more and more complex so far we've already added these probabilities in here. And also we've added the discounting factor. Now we're going to look in more detail at this side of the question where we have the reward now. Remember previously when we talked about how reinforcement learning works we said we have an agent and it performs actions in the environment and in an exchange or as a result of that it gets a new state and which is now in and a reward for that action. Well so far in our example we've only been getting rewards at the very end either if we get to the finish line or if we for the agent ends up in the fire pit he gets a plus one or a minus one reward. But that is a very simplistic approach to reinforcement learning and in more realistic scenarios you will likely have rewards throughout the journey not just at the very end you might have rewards throughout the journey. For instance if it's an AI playing a game and if for example it's like shooting somebody in doom it might get points for killing that enemy or it might be a different other game. If it overtakes another car or something like that just because of the rules of the game not because of its way of analyzing the game but actually the game is structured in a way that it's reinforcing its giving points for doing certain actions even before the game is over. So Sinatras like that are very common and not just in games and also in real life and that's why we're going to introduce something similar into our example a simplified version of that but nevertheless a reward that is continuously given to the agent throughout the game not just at the end and the way we're going to do it is by looking at the other tiles. So right now we only have a reward plus one at the final tile and reward minus 1 at the other final tile, the firepit. But now we're going to add rewards every single time. We'll add a very small reward which will be minus 0.04.

"Living Penalty"

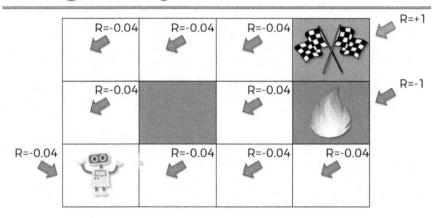

And as you can see it's negative so every time the agent moves he'll get a negative reward and that's called a living penalty because no matter where he goes he will always get this negative reward except for these final tiles because that's the end of the game. And so you can see the reward even on this tile is madness or a puzzle. But that doesn't mean that he starts with that reward. He only gets this reward. And this is important to remember he only gets his reward when he enters a tile so whenever he promises an action he goes here then he will get this reward minus 0.04 and then when he comes back to this style he'll get another mind and 0.04 word. And so the longer he walks around the more he accumulates his negative reward and therefore is an incentive for him to finish the game earlier so quickly as possible. And so now let's have a look at how our policy or how the agent's policy is going to change depending on what value we set for this reward. So here are four environments and in each one we're going to explore a different one. We're not going to do the calculations. We're just going to project the results and you will see that intuitively they make total sense. So here we've got a reward for any step offered for getting into any state. Is equal to zero. Just as what we've seen before here, the reward is going to be Mei's 0.0. For what we just did just now you know the reward will be at minus 0.5 or the level of giving penalty will be mine is open fire so much higher you can see them here more than 10 times greater. And here in Penhall it will be minus two. So even more than the rewards you get for jumping or even less than the reward that you are the agent gets for ending up in the fire pit. So let's have a look at how the actions or the optimal policy for passing this environment will change depending on this reward. So this is our original policy. And as you can remember we had these two very interesting and even a little bit weird decisions by the agent but which totally makes sense if he can live for as long as he likes. If you can just travel around for as long as he wants without being penalized for staying alive very long. He why not why wouldn't he just go into the corner here into the wall and just keep doing that until it happens. It so happens that he goes this way and then he will walk around. And same thing here it's much safer for him to jump into the wall hoping that one of these will come up eventually and then he'll go to the finish line anyway because by choosing these two actions he doesn't risk getting into the fire pit. Now let's see what happens if we add a negative reward for just being a life for making a step. Move here you can see that instantly these two changed. Now the agent doesn't want to jump into the wall. He is more likely to risk getting to the firepit having a 10 percent chance of jumping in here but he will go forward because every time he comes to watch here if he was going to be doing it here as well every time he jumps into well he performs an action he ends up into in this state with an 80 percent chance. And that means an 80 percent chance you'll get a minus 0.04 reward meaning that a lot of the time he's going to be accumulating this negative reward. Same thing here if he jumps into the wall waiting for that moment when he will actually be randomly moved to the right. If he keeps doing that he will accumulate this negative reward and that the result of that if you perform the calculations you'll see that the result of that the expected value of that approach jumping to the wall is worse than taking the risk of going forward and actually ending up in the firepit. So he changes his decisions in these two blocks to instead move forward and here move to the left even though there's a risk of the firepit fire simply because now the longer he's alive the longer he will accumulate this living penalty in the next environment. Now we're increasing the living Pouncey to even a greater number Meinzer point five and let's see what changes here. So now you can see that compared to this environment. The only thing that changed here is that this arrow is pointing to the right. And what that means is that now it's no longer a good option for the agent or actually also this arrow pointing was pointing the left and nozzle's nose pointing upwards. So now it's no longer a good idea for the agent to go around from here or go around all the way because if he goes wrong all the way yes he's safe or there's a lesser chance there's no chance of getting the fire pit. But at the same time there's less chance of it happening. But at the same time he will accumulate quite a substantial negative reward as he walks around. So it's just that the path is too long. So that forces him whether he's here or here to take the shorter route to get here even though he has a much higher risk of getting into the fire pit because as soon as he ends up in the square there's a 10 percent chance of getting to the fire. According to his calculations. It's just the expected value of this approach is better than the expected value of going around simply because we've increased this living penalty. And finally we're getting to the example with the living penalty of minus two point zero. So here I encourage you to post the video now that you've seen how the policy has changed as we increase the loading punt penalty. I encourage you to pause the video and think for yourself what will happen in this scenario. What do you think the optimal policy will be given that the living penalty is so high so all this supposed video if you'd like to. And now I'm going to jump into showing you the solution so in this case if you increase the penalty to minus 2.0 it's so high remember that the penalty here is only minus 1.0 it's so high that the agent just wants to get out of the game in any way possible even if it's just by jumping into the fire pit. He will do it. He will be like every time I make a step every time I end up in a new place in your state or every time I make an action I end up getting a minus two reward. So what's the point of trying to get to the finish line if from here will take me two extra steps. I'm just going to go here and then straight into the fire pit because that way my reward is going to be less than negative reward is going to be as bad as in the case of just making additional steps so you can see that adding this living reward and depending on the value of the living reward that we're adding the results are going to be different.

"Living Penalty"

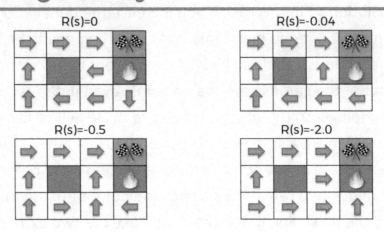

And the agent is going to select different policies and that's basically what's how the reward value can be incorporated by the Belmont equation even when it's not just at the finish line or at the end of the game but even throughout the game. And again once again doesn't have to be on every single in every single state depending on the environment itself. It might be given to the agent at certain specific states, not at every state but in our simplistic example we're just using rewards at every given state. To illustrate this concept, I hope you enjoyed today's project. And as you can see we've already made our Bellman equation quite sophisticated and now it can be applied to many different scenarios and I can't wait to see in the next project.

Q-LEARNING INTUITION

Today we are finally talking about Kule learning. All right so we've already got this equation the bellman equation which we've added lots of components to. We've got the reward here which can be not just at the very end but it can be at any given step. We've got the discount factor. We've got the probability because now we're looking at the mark of a decision process. And here we've got the possibility of ending up in a different state regardless of what action we take or actually given the action we take. There can be multiple states that we can end up in and then we get the value of the next states because he kind of like a recursive function and so on but you probably still have one question. The question is where in all of this is no letter Q Why is it all called q. Learning. So where's the cue? And that's the question that we're going to be answering today. So far we've been dealing with values the value of being in a certain state and now we're going to look at how Q fits into all of that as well. So here we've got two examples on the left of what we would be doing so far our agent has been analyzing. Ok I'm over here. This is a mark of the decision process so it doesn't matter how I got here. The rest of the environment doesn't care about the steps that it took me to get here from now on. I have to make the optimal decision where to go here or here. Based on the current state and all the future states that come from here but not from the past. And so he can see that there's three options: there's one state to state three. And based on his experience he has calculated the values in these states and now he's going to use the bellman equation. So even though this is a classic Proceso he knows that he'll go here but there's a chance that he will go left right and so on. So based on these values going to make a decision that's what we do so far and that is a totally legitimate approach here. But now we're getting modified a little bit. We're going to take the same exact concept, same exact problem but here instead of looking at the values of each state that he can end up in we're going to look at the values or the value of each action. So we're not going to use the letter V anymore because for the value of the state we're going to use a Q and then you might have a question why the letter Q Well. Q Some people speculate that. Q Will I read this? I think on Quora. Somebody mentioned that Q is because of quality but at the same time I couldn't find any other references to that so it might not be because that might just because that's the letter that was used at the time and now it became super popular because it's all called key learning because of that. So no exact reason was held. Q But nevertheless at least it helps us distinguish between V and Q So Q here. There were presents rather than the value of the state it represents. It represents the quality of the action that represents. OK so I've got four actions. What are the different qualities of these actions? What is the value of the action or the quality of the action? Which action is more lucrative? I need a metric telling me all right. How do I quantify this action and then I can compare them and that is exactly what Q is. And so he's got four possible actions. As always, go up right, left or down. And based on the action there's going to be a formula which tells us the quantifiable value of that action which we're calling the Q q value of that action.

Q-Learning Intuition

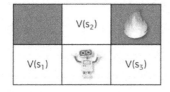 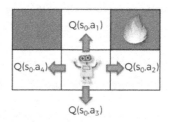

So let's have a look at how we are going to derive this formula. Q What does it actually relate to ? Because as you can imagine because actions lead to states there has to be some sort of link between the two. Right we've got we've already determined how to calculate this and we're pretty good at it. We know how to use the Bellman equation in very different environments with lots of different complications. Well let's leverage that knowledge to understand how we can now calculate. Q In order to make the same predictions because as you can imagine the environment doesn't change depending on what approach we use the environment is going to be the same regardless. So therefore this approach and this approach should always give the same result and therefore that's another reason why these two should be linked. So let's have a look. So here is our view approach where we just get to look at the value of any given state, this state or any other state. And here we go into we're just using the lead here because that's the current state. And so therefore the terminology will be the same in both equations and here we are using q as a Q Is the of the state s and the action. A because action is up but in which state we perform that action we perform that action in the State. OK so now we're going to ride out the Bellman equation for the first approach as you can see here we've got the of s or the value of any given state s is the maximum of the reward that you get a maximum bet based on the actions you have. In this case you actually have four actions so maxim out of all the possible actions of this part which we've heard discussed many times so this is our reward that we get from performing that action in that state plaza discount in fact multiplied by the expected value of the new state that we're going to be in an expected value because it is a stochastic process. We don't know exactly for sure that we're going to end up here . We might end up on the left or the right sort of probability. That's why these probabilities are in you. All right so that's our value. And now let's look at. Q So Q is going to be defined. We're going to use this to define Q So let's say the agent from this location from this state performs the action up. What is the q value going to be called to. Well first of all let's see what he will get in return for performing this action up. First thing that you'll get is a reward right. No doubt about it. There's going to be some sort of rule or might be zero but we know that the whole way this reinforcement learning process works is that some towns are performing certain actions from a given state or two. So I'm going to add that here. And then we're going to add what we are going to add. Well let's think about it. What is the next thing that happens after he's going there? Well next thing that happens is that now the agent is in a certain state he could end up here with a 80 percent probability or some probability. But actually up here right here. But wherever he ends up now there's we already have a quantified metric for that state he's in. And that is actually the value of that state. But because he came up in many different states and three of the possible different states we have to look at the expected value of the state that he'll be in. And so we're going to add that in. Of course the discounted factor as we previously had because that is somewhere in the future. And then we're going to add the some of across all possible states across all possible states that he could end up by taking this action. Terms of probability. So what we're saying here is that OK so by performing an action you're going to get a reward Plus which is a quantified metric Plus you're going to get. You end up in a state where we don't know which one it could be here. Could be here it could be here. But here is the expected value of the state that you're going to end up in. And now we're going to multiply by discounting factor because that is one move away. So that is our Q value for this for the performance section and what you will notice here right away is that. Q The Q value is actually exactly identical to what's inside these brackets over here. And why is that? Well if you think about it here we're taking the maximum of the results and will get the maximum across all possible actions so we got the maximum across all possible actions of the result that we'll get by taking each of those actions and the enqueue we're defining. Interesting. What will we get by taking a certain action? So if you think about it it makes sense that the value of a state.

Q-Learning Intuition

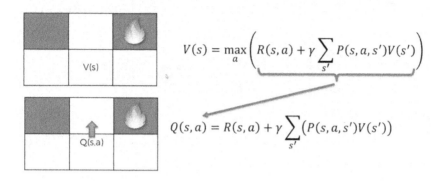

$$V(s) = \max_{a}\left(R(s,a) + \gamma \sum_{s'} P(s,a,s')V(s')\right)$$

$$Q(s,a) = R(s,a) + \gamma \sum_{s'} (P(s,a,s')V(s'))$$

So for instance this state is the maximum of all of the possible Q values. Right here in the States by being in the state the agent has one key value to keep the 3Q value for q value. So yes positive for possible Q values while the value of the stay makes sense that the value of the state is the maximum of all of those four key values. That is exactly what we can see here. That's a good confirmation of this new formula that we derive. If that wasn't the case if that didn't match up then we would have questions. So why doesn't it match. Why doesn't it match up if. Q value is a quantified metric of performing an action and V depends on the floor. Is like the maximum of the possible results of the four actions that he can perform over that makes sense. And that confirms the formula that we've just derived and now we're going to make it even more interesting. We're going to get rid of the Wii entirely because you can see here you've got the Wii as a recursive function. So and then you've got me and then B and then B and then B and so on. So you can express this view through all of the following Vee's: the most optimal will come up here. We're expecting Q As a funk a recursive function of the OR as a function of the next V and then you'd have to plug in this V and then we get back to the B. So what are we going to do is we're actually going to take this V and we're going to we're going to replace it with Q Right so let's have a look at that. We're going to take this V of the next state and we're going to plug this into that formula over here. And as you can see now so this part doesn't change this probability doesn't change. But as we just discussed, the s is the maximum by all actions of q of S and right over here. So that's what we're going to replace here. So we're going to say a maximum of course is the new action the action that we're going to take because here we've got the Wii of as prime. So here now we've got the maximal console at a prime. So the actions that we're going to take from this state are from wherever whichever other state we end up in but the action we're going to take from there and Maxima across all those and the maximum is of all the cube values that will that are available to us in that new state as prime comma a prime. And that's action. So that's it. So there's going to be another four. Q values there. So now as you can see let's go through again. So as from what we derive this word would be just cause just through logic and intuition so that we can see that VNS are actually the view of AS and of and a are linked. The S is the maximum across all actions of Cuba S and you can see right here so this part is identical to this part. And then we're going to leverage that and we're going to replace this bit with VNS from here but not this exact funnel we're going to take this internal part and replace it with kill the innocent. So we're going to plug that in here and this part is going to be q of s prime a prime maximum of cube by Crucell a Priam's of Q As Prime a prime. And now we have our formula. So now we have a recursive formula for the q value so now the agent can think what's the value of the section, what's the quality of this section and the new value of this action. Well it depends on the reward I get in the immediate step after that plus it depends on the discounted factor times the maximum of all the possible Q actions in that state. But I don't know if I'm going to get their side needed to also look at that state in that state and that's why we have this expected value over here so we have some probability times the maximum that's expected value. So a very similar formula as you can see but this time we're expressing things through the q values and that's why this whole algorithm is called Kill learning because this is what is looked at this is what the agents actually use they don't look at the states look at their possible actions and then based on the actions on the q value of the actions they will decide which action to take. So they'll just look at the maximum

Q value in this given state; it has four actions. What is the best action to take so it can compare the different states that it can end up in is going to compare the possible actions that it currently has then by finding the optimal one is going to take that action and then engage is going to repeat that process repeat that process and so on. So now you can see how all this comes together how the reward the discounting facts or the stochastic market decision processes and the values and the q values all come together in order to cueist this one super powerful Bellman equation for q values which we can now apply and let our agents learn how to beat the environment. And so that is an intuitive explanation of what's going on. I know we went through the formulas but it is necessary because this is like our formula that's we've been going through this whole chapter and I think it's a good transition from the To. Q And it illustrates how there are links between Yishun And if you'd like to get a bit more of a rigorous mathematical approach and like you see the mathematics behind it and learn a bit more about q values and how they work. Then we've got some additional reading for you. This paper is called Markov decision processes concepts and algorithms by Martin von Autor low 2009. So you cut the link here as always and here you can read in a bit more detail to understand all the nitty gritty behind Hugh values and so on and now that we've discussed all of these things relating to the Bellman equation now we are ready to look at something more complex such as this paper in order if if we want to get some additional information on this in order to kind of get a deeper understanding. But even if you don't read the newspaper or radio you should have a good working knowledge of what learning is all about and how agents come up with the actions that they need to take in a certain environment.

TEMPORAL DIFFERENCE

Today we're talking about the temporal difference. Now it's very important to trial because temporal difference is the heart and soul of the Q learning algorithm. This is actually how everything we've learned so far comes together into play inside key learning. So let's have a look. Remember the time when we talked about deterministic versus nondeterministic search. And remember how we said in this case it's when the agent wants to go up he goes up and when. In this case if he wants to go up there's a 10 percent chance he'll go lower left temps and chance and go right and an 80 percent chance will go right. Go straight up. While these numbers are of course arbitrary and can be different. And this whole concept is it could be different and different problems so it doesn't have to concern which way he's moving, just that there's some randomness, something that's out of the control of the agent happening inside this environment. And what effect that had is as you remember was that in the deterministic example it was very easy to calculate the

Wii values while not necessarily always very easy. But in our case we could just simply calculate them by using the Bellman equation and we had the exact values. And then as you remember I very carefully mentioned that these values for the nondeterministic search example are off the top of my head. They are not the Kalka we know. Last time I said we're not, we just had to calculate them because it's very complex. But the computer can do it and we just went along with these values that are just values that I made up. But they did get the job done. They helped us understand the concept. Well now we're going to return to that a little bit and understand what exactly is going on here. Why is it so much harder to calculate these values in the nondeterministic example or generally speaking in these problems in these environments and the agent going through them. Why is it? Why can it be so hard to calculate these values? Well when you think about it because when the agent moves for instance from here to the right he doesn't necessarily always move that way sometimes as a chance that he will go to win instead of going straight so let's call this northeast southwest so it sort of goes west. The agent might sometimes go south and for instance from here is sort of going north. He might sometimes go east. So sorry. So here instead of going east he might sometimes go south and he's sort of going north. He might sometimes go east or west and here instead of going north he might sometimes go west or east or west and so on. So in order to calculate this value you would need to know what this value is but the interesting thing is that in order to calculate this value you need to know what this value is. So there's a lot of recursion happening here and therefore you cannot just decide to define what these values are. And on top of that this recursion is not deterministic. Sometimes it happens this way. Sometimes it's sort of uphill to go right sometimes instead of getting up and going left sometimes. When he wants to go up. He will go up. So it is subject to chance and so maybe many times agent will go through this path and he'll go up up up up up and you'll think that from here you always kind of goes up and the value of the state will go it will be good and then all of a sudden he'll drop into the pit and this value will go down. And so therefore you can see how there is some stochastic randomness to this whole calculation on these values because they're all interlinked. Plus on top you've got that randomness inherent in the environment because there's a mark of the decision process. So that's where all this comes together and that's where we're going to introduce the concept of the temporal difference which will allow the agent to calculate these values. And here we were dealing with the values. And since then we've already moved onto Q values so that's what we're going to be working on.

Temporal Difference

V=0.71	V=0.74	V=0.86	🏁
V=0.63		V=0.39	🔥
V=0.55	V=0.46	V=0.36	V=0.22

We're going to be looking at huge values. So as I recall this is our Bellman equation for q values. So AQ value or the value of performing a sort of action A in state s is equal to the reward that you get after performing that action immediately after performing an action plus do you get the maximum you get the gamma of the sum of all the possible. So you kind of get the expected value of the state that you will end up in. So as you recall there was a formula for the Beldon equation and now just for simplicity say we're going to rewrite it in the old fashioned way and in a way that we used to talk about the bellman equation before we knew about the sequester. So remember this was our Bellman equation in the sense of a deterministic search example because here you don't have that expected value you don't have the same across all probabilities. You just have that as if it's determined you're going to end up in what state you're going to end up in and then you tell Max in that one state. And the reason we're rewriting it is simply the only reason is because it is just easier to write it and it'll be easier to fall along with the formula. So we're going to just remember that we replaced this part of this bar. And also you'll find this notation in a lot of literature so it'll be easier for you to follow along with other sources if you're studying those. But do remember that in fact what we mean is this probabilistic approach here instead of this notation is just easier for us to operate this and understand what's going on. I just kind of like to look at the equations so that they're not too cluttered but once again just remember that in fact what we mean is this probabilistic approach here. And so we're actually in the know. Tom Silis has a look at what's going on. So here is our blank state of the maze. We don't have any q values let's see or when we may but let's just keep it blank for now let's just look at one of the states or one of the cells. This one specifically. And here we have for answers for the action of going up. We have a q value that we calculate. So it's not that we don't have any q values yet we have it we do. But we're just not illustrating anything. We're just keeping a blank for simplicity's sake. But we have been walking around for some time and let's say hypothetically somehow he's calculated this cube value of going up or Norf from this state from this specific cell and the values. Q S and A and so now what we have. So he is currently with his blue arrows point and the agent is sitting in this cell. And now he needs to make a choice where he is going to go. And he knows the value of this action going north and that is q Senay and here I'm saying before and the reason for that is because he that is before he takes Actually he hasn't taken action yet so he's still in the cell and before he's taken the action the value here is q and SNH and now he actually takes the action. So let's say he decides it is the best one. He takes the action and he moves up to the cell. Well now what happens is now comes after so after he's taken action we can measure what is this value let's just calculate this value the value of the reward for taking that action plus gamma times the maximum of this new state that he's just gotten into as prime. And so the maximum across all possible actions and aspirin. And so what we have here is the value before that action. And then we calculated this metric afterwards. But as you can recall from the previous four months if we go back very quickly from the previous formula where we just calculated is indeed the value that is how Q of s.a.a is calculated. So this Arite part is just calculated separately but after we've taken action. So as again before we knew a Q of an S and a value something that we've calculated through our iterations Preuss is something. So a value that's stored in our memory. So just like a number that we know and now after the action is being performed we know what reward he actually got and what reward the agent actually got. And we can calculate this new value. So in essence we're kind of recalculating this value but now with new information the new information is the reward that we got. And plus what stayed we ended up in and what the maximum across that state is that this new value is for that specific data can. So what's the value of that being in that state. So basically the Cure Vanessa-Mae but given new information and now the temporal difference is defined as tiddy of a and s of these two of the difference between these two. So here the first element is your off-Terra value. So the Q of Esson is a bit calculated afterwards. And the previous quvenzhanE which you had stored in your memory. And so the question is are they different. So ideally they should be the same. Ideally this should be the same as this simply because this is the formula for calculating this. But the thing is that this is not something we Kalka, this is something that we have from empirical evidence, something that we have from just going through the maze many times and calculating. So this is something we came up with so far. It's not related to the current iteration. It's something that we came up with previously a long long time ago but in one of our previous iterations going through the maze. Whereas this is something we've calculated just now and there is no guarantee that they're going to be the same or because of the randomness that exists in the maze because this could have been calculated and saw some CRN random events were triggered and this can be called to different random events happening were triggered.

Temporal Difference

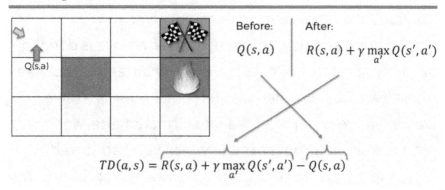

Before:

$$Q(s, a)$$

After:

$$R(s, a) + \gamma \max_{a'} Q(s', a')$$

$$TD(a, s) = R(s, a) + \gamma \max_{a'} Q(s', a') - Q(s, a)$$

And so now we write down our heroes just move it up there. So how do we use this? The question is OK so we have this temporal difference. How do we use this? And why is it called the temporal difference? Well the reason is called the temporal difference is because you're basically calculating the same thing you're calculating Q of S and A so the Q value of that action. Your Calcott here and you're calculating it here. But the difference is time. This is the Q of S and they previously this is yo Q of S and A. Now your new cure is innate and the question is has there been a difference. Has there been a shift between them in time? And how can we use this to our advantage if there indeed has been a shift in time. Well one thing we could do is we could say OK well you know our Q of s.a.a doesn't. This new value doesn't equal old so we are going to get rid of the old or forget about the old and we'll just use this as a new value. But that would not be smart. And the reason for that is that in our environments random events can sometimes happen. And what if our old QSA of s.a.a was something that consistently happens like 80 percent of the time. And then like was represented by what happens 80 percent of the time. And then this new one just happened due to randomness. In that case we're going to throw away the one that is responsible for the bulk of the situation and we're going to replace it with something that happens only 10 or 20 percent of the time. That wouldn't be the best approach to go and that's why that's exactly why we don't want to completely change Opu values. We want to change them step by step a little bit by a little bit. And that's why we're going to use this temporal difference in a specific way so we're going to say Here's a formula we're going to take our cue of SNH. And we're going to update it in such a way. We're going to take the old value of cure Senay and we are going to add all five times the temporal difference. So Alpha is going to be all learning right. That's a new parameter that we're introducing. That's how quickly algorithm learning is. So basically we're taking this difference and whatever it is we're adding it on to our previous KJo snake. Now this formula probably doesn't make any sense or like just by looking it doesn't make sense because you got Covisint here and give us an A here. It's the same thing so probably we should negate each other but we had to rewrite this in a bit of a different way. So I'm going to show you again so I'm just adding time to these formulas. So here is q t minus one the previous years. Q T minus 1 the previous years. Q T The New this should be a circle here in a circle here as well but never mind and here get alpha temporal difference. Then you know the current temporal difference. So you can see what we're doing. OK let's take our current. Q is going to be equal to all previous Q plus whatever temporal difference we found Times Alpha. This formula here is the heart and soul of the cube learning algorithm. This is how the cube is or updated. And it's good that we've already learned what q values are, what gamma is , and what all this stuff is. And now all we need to see is that you have a previous Q value. Yes, that's good. And then what can happen is that when you take in when you actually do take the action when the agent takes action you'll know he'll get a reward and he'll end up in a state. And so based on that he can calculate Aha. OK so what is what would have been the Q value of that move that I made. And now that is this part of the equation. Subtracting the old Q value gets you a temporal difference and now you need to take an Alpher time sample difference and that's how you get adjusted. Q Got you, that's what you mean. I just think you go by and now just to finish off this. This is kind of like this is sufficient to understand what's going on but just to clarify things even more or perhaps maybe confuse things even more. What do we need to do to take this temporal difference or this simple difference or here a way to plug it into this format. So we're going to take all of this part and plug it into this formula and end up with a huge equation. So here we go. There's our equation. So this is the full equation with the temporal difference written out completely. And the reason I wrote it out as well first of all you'll probably find this in other literature if you study it. And the second thing is that it makes some things a bit more complex and formulas longer but also makes some things a bit clearer. So for instance you can see here the role Alpha plays. You can see it better because look at this. Here. Q T minus one and here you go. Q T minus one with a negative sign. So if you plug in Alpha equals to 1 if you put a 1 in here then this will negate this. So they'll destroy each other and all you'll have left is this part. And what that means is exactly that situation where we said All right so you've got a new value which it should have been. Let's update our Q value with the new value and forget about whatever we had previously. And as we discussed, this isn't the best approach because there are random events here and we want to update things step by step. And on other hand if you said Alpher equal to zero what happens then is that you completely forget about this whole part and you're cute to the new one or the current one is going to be always equal to the previous one so you're not going to be learning anything. And that means whatever is happening in the maze doesn't matter because you've decided on your Kuchi value a long time ago and you're just going to keep it. So that's why Alfas shouldn't be 0 or should be one it should be somewhere in between. And it's going to allow you to learn slowly step by step. It is going to allow you to ask your or the agent as it goes through the maze. It is going to get the temporal difference. And slowly but surely this value is going to get updated and updated and what will happen eventually is that at some point hopefully the algorithm will converge. And what that means is that this temporal difference will start becoming closer and closer to zero and eventually will be just well very close to zero or even 0 0 0 0 and what that means is that every single time your new cutesie value or your new calculated value. What it should have been. So not this one but what it hypothetically should be enough to take the step will be just equal to your previous Q2 value. And then one that's zero and that means when your temperature difference is zero means your algorithm has converged and it's not really necessary to continue updating what's going on. It does this search to continue updating your cube values. The caveat here is that the only time is probably one of the only times when you would still want to continue performing this whole you know updating of queue values if the environment is constantly changing. If not just it's not there it just has some random Kostic events in it. But the environment itself is modifying as morphing is changing with time. So you continuously need to learn because it's not possible for you to learn everything and come up with the optimal policy because the optimal policies also change with the environment all the time. In that case you will need to continue CALKIN and temporal difference and calculate the Q values. But other than that that's kind of like an extra complication. Other than that this is how Q values update is so this is the main formula of the Q learning algorithm and this is kind of like the expanded version of that and now it should all come together and make sense why we have the Bellman equation and not only what it represents the gewgaws but also how the agent goes about updating its values and finding exactly what is going on in that environment so it can come up with the optimal policy.

Temporal Difference

$$TD_t(a, s) = R(s, a) + \gamma \max_{a'} Q(s', a') - Q_{t-1}(s, a)$$

$$Q_t(s, a) = Q_{t-1}(s, a) + \alpha TD_t(a, s)$$

$$Q_t(s, a) = Q_{t-1}(s, a) + \alpha \left(R(s, a) + \gamma \max_{a'} Q(s', a') - Q_{t-1}(s, a) \right)$$

So I know quite a lot to take in but hopefully you enjoyed this project and hopefully you able to take away the underlying concepts and intuition behind your values and what's the whole notion of temporal difference is and why it's important why it helps us slowly train our agents and get them to understand their environments that they're operating in. And if you'd like to learn a bit more about temporal differences then a very popular paper is learning to predict by the methods of temporal differences by Richard Sutton of nineteen eighty eight.

Additional Reading

Additional Reading:

Learning to Predict by the Methods of Temporal Differences

By Richard Sutton (1988)

Link:

https://link.springer.com/article/10.1007/BF00115009

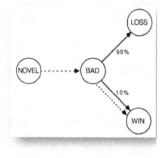

We've already had a reference by Richard Sutton as well but this is as another one and actually has a book so if you get into you know his writing style and his style of communication then check out his book as well. It is kind of like a more expanded version of all of these things. I haven't read the book but that's what I'm imagining at the same time. This is going to add to the paper and you can learn a bit more about or probably a lot more about temporal differences there.

Q-LEARNING VISUALIZATION

In today's project we're going to have some fun. We're going to have a look and artificial intelligence is actually going through that maze that we've been talking about so long and is going to use kill learning to navigate its way and find the way out and we'll see what happens to the q values and what is going to happen to the policy and so on. So let's have a look. We're going to be using some materials kindly provided by Berkeley University. So if you go to a I don't Birk only the E R K E L E Why don't you just go to that link again. You'll see this Web site and hear what we're going to be looking at is the need to go to PacMan projects. I think Pacman projects and here if you scroll down and you look at them on first learning this is what we're working with. So here you can download the zip archive. So that's if you want to. So don't you don't have to do this if we're not going to go through a solution together in this trial just letting you know where this is all from because we're very similar. We really appreciate that. UC Berkeley has made these materials available. But if you do wish to experiment with this on your own. Just bear in mind this is not part. Is not going to be part of our courses as part of the Berkeley course. I'm not sure how it works for illustration purposes but if you do want to experiment with this you can find it here the zip archive and all old instructions as well. And we're just going to go into Python right away and the first thing I wanted to show you is that here we've got the licensing information so this is what I mean. We're very lucky that they said we are free to use or extend these projects for educational purposes provided you know distributing publish solutions which we're not going to do. You retain this notice which we have and you provide a clear archbishop to UC Berkeley including a link to which we also have. So once again if you'd like to learn more there is a link. You can have a look. And thank you very much all of these people who have worked on this project so here's the grid world. We're going to be working if there is a solution there.

You would have to in order to make it work you'd have to solve it yourself or possibly find a solution. Maybe some of your some people somebody you know might help you out with that. If again what you want to you don't have to because we are just going to look at it on this screen right now. So after we've created all those files we could just launch it over here. So there are some parameters that are involved in this whole world and we're not going to just show you what it looks like if we launch it. So let's try to launch it in manual mode. So if I go minus one of these panoramas are manual so I can command your control agent. So here you can see all the grids so I can go up so you can see that it's taking action starting and starting in the states where I was. And then you saw that I pressed up, took action Norf and the first time I ended up zero once I did go up. But the second time I took action Norf and I ended up in the same sad state. So something happened. You know, randomness happened. I either went left or right. And by default the parameters are set. You can see here by default they're set to exactly what we discussed and that often actually results in an unintended direction. 20 percent of the time to 10 percent to the left, some to the right. So if I go up and say I went up I go right. I went right now and it didn't happen. Right again and right and I'm finished. But in this implementation you have to click again to get out of this final output so out of there just click again and you're finished. That's a terminal state so we can run our manual. You can see that if I go right right right left up. So here what we saw previously was that the agent wouldn't go straight up right. What's the point of going up if there's a chance of going into the pit? So let's see what the agent would do. It would go left and go west here would go West. And you see I clicked left but it went up and here I would click right. And I end up in the final exit stage and you see God's reward equal to one. So that's what it looks like manually. Now let's actually hook up an AI to this and let it go through. So let's do an H here and let's add some Brandner. So let me just see what I typed here so hopefully you can see by grid world why then here minus our means. That's the reward for living. So I've got two of them so I probably should remove this one. So minus k is how many iterations. That's way too many iterations. Let's do less. Let's do like 10 iterations should be enough. Minus a is Agent.

```
Command Prompt                                                    ___ _ _
Started in state: <3, 0>
Took action: west
Ended in state: <2, 0>
Got reward: 0.0

Started in state: <2, 0>
Took action: north
Ended in state: <2, 1>
Got reward: 0.0

Started in state: <2, 1>
Took action: west
Ended in state: <2, 2>
Got reward: 0.0

Started in state: <2, 2>
Took action: east
Ended in state: <3, 2>
Got reward: 0.0

Started in state: <3, 2>
Took action: exit
Ended in state: TERMINAL_STATE
Got reward: 1

C:\Users\Kirill\.spyder\Reinforcement>python GridWorld.py -h
Usage: GridWorld.py [options]

Options:
  -h, --help            show this help message and exit
  -d DISCOUNT, --discount=DISCOUNT
                        Discount on future (default 0.9)
  -r R, --livingReward=R
                        Reward for living for a time step (default 0.0)
  -n P, --noise=P       How often action results in unintended direction
                        (default 0.2)
  -e E, --epsilon=E     Chance of taking a random action in q-learning
                        (default 0.3)
  -l P, --learningRate=P
                        TD learning rate (default 0.5)
  -i K, --iterations=K  Number of rounds of value iteration (default 10)
  -k K, --episodes=K    Number of epsiodes of the MDP to run (default 1)
  -g G, --grid=G        Grid to use (case sensitive; options are BookGrid,
                        BridgeGrid, CliffGrid, MazeGrid, default BookGrid)
  -w X, --windowSize=X  Request a window width of X pixels *per grid cell*
                        (default 150)
  -a A, --agent=A       Agent type (options are 'random', 'value' and 'q',
                        default random)
  -t, --text            Use text-only ASCII display
  -p, --pause           Pause GUI after each time step when running the MDP
  -q, --quiet           Skip display of any learning episodes
  -s S, --speed=S       Speed of animation, S > 1.0 is faster, 0.0 < S < 1.0
                        is slower (default 1.0)
  -m, --manual          Manually control agent
  -v, --valueSteps      Display each step of value iteration

C:\Users\Kirill\.spyder\Reinforcement>python GridWorld.py -r -0.4 -k 1000 -a q -
s 20000 -r -0.04 -d 1_
```

What type of agent don't want to do honor and image
and some value or a Q. Q So I want a Q. Q learning agent
doing this minus s is what is s speed so that's way too
large a force that just use the full speed for now minus R
is a living penalty's so by default is zero. So remember at
the very start restart 0 living penances so let's call it also 0
0 and can just remove this parameter and D is what is d

discount. So I just kind of factor so let's keep it at zero point and so very similar to what we're starting off in this section on the course so let's run that OK way too fast again all actually so pretty OK so you can see how he's exploring. And so far he's hit negative three times and you can see how the q values are being updated in these squares. So these are key values. They are sort of zero. You can see the Q value now. So he's learned that this one is a bit different to implement because once you get to the final stage you have to get out of it. You have to just click one more button to exit. And so it's very close to one but not exactly one. But at the same time you can see that here you know the value slowly, kind of crystallizing hands are a point of an ex-colleague getting somewhere but they're just so far they're kind of zeroes because he doesn't have enough information to understand what's going on. OK so let's see, let's see what happens here. Exploring exploring exploring what's going to happen. Well, it's been a while. And we get some randomness involved here. So there is that good one a few times. Now he only gets 10 iterations. So he's got to learn fast. Ok I need you there. Let's see what's going on. Come on. Get out of that maze already. And yes 10 episodes so average it turns out that. I'm not really interested in that. So here let's see. I've never seen enough of a click. Right. There we go. So you can see this is the policy that he came up with. Even through just 10 episodes he's already got a pulse. I'm going to go up a bomb and here I'm going to go down here I'm going to go down here I'm going to go into the wall and then I'm going to bounce we're here. That's pretty cool. OK. So now let's increase the speed. What were the parameters there? And that's like double lawlessness. That's quadruple the speed and let's increase the number of iterations so let's say 20 to ration this time and let's see if he can get through a bit more now. So you can see he's going a bit faster. And he's learning he's learning that it's not really you know out of this state there's not many good actions Orio these actions that the right and straight are not that good. This was definitely not good. He still needs to learn that so from here is also good.

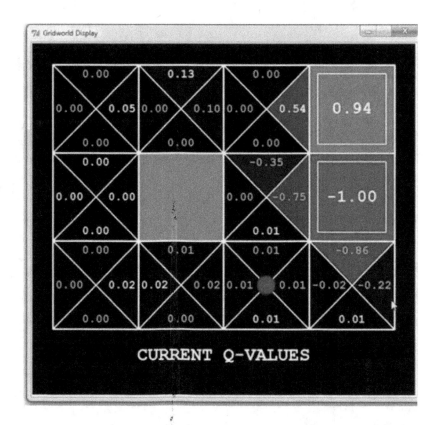

CURRENT Q-VALUES

```
Started in state: (2, 2)
Took action: east
Ended in state: (3, 2)
Got reward: 0.0

Started in state: (3, 2)
Took action: exit
Ended in state: TERMINAL_STATE
Got reward: 1

EPISODE 17 COMPLETE: RETURN WAS 0.531441

BEGINNING EPISODE: 18

Started in state: (0, 0)
Took action: east
Ended in state: (1, 0)
Got reward: 0.0

Started in state: (1, 0)
Took action: east
Ended in state: (2, 0)
Got reward: 0.0

Started in state: (2, 0)
Took action: east
Ended in state: (3, 0)
Got reward: 0.0

Started in state: (3, 0)
Took action: north
Ended in state: (3, 1)
Got reward: 0.0

Started in state: (3, 1)
Took action: exit
Ended in state: TERMINAL_STATE
Got reward: -1

EPISODE 18 COMPLETE: RETURN WAS -0.6561

BEGINNING EPISODE: 19

Started in state: (0, 0)
Took action: east
Ended in state: (1, 0)
Got reward: 0.0

Started in state: (1, 0)
Took action: east
Ended in state: (2, 0)
Got reward: 0.0

Started in state: (2, 0)
Took action: south
Ended in state: (2, 0)
Got reward: 0.0
```

You can see that this action is pretty good. All right. What did he get? OK. So interesting policy here you decide to go up. Just not enough information. So let's really do that. And let's increase the speed to like 100. Super fast and the number of iterations will give him 100 iterations this time it's run that scene like crazy fast and you can see that because there's so many more iterations He's got more information more opportunity to experiment and to actually build out this this matrix or matrix these values for every single state. He now knows you can see that zero point eighty nine. What did we say in our zero point 86. Another thing to remember is the value of any given state. Remember that formula we had is the maximum of the cube values. Remember that we came up with a shortcut formula. So what is it with the value in this state being the V of this. It would be 0.18. Because that's the highest out of the four here the value of this state 0.7 you want the value of this day. There is a point sixty one and so on. So that's something to remember. I remember when I was up I think we had like zero point 86 or something so praecox. And so if we go next year I'll just disappear or disappear again and this can make it come back. OK. OK. Slowly slowly slowly filling up some spaces. I see. And it's also pretty random because not only the environment has randomness but also the way he explores that the star really doesn't know the policy is he's exploring at random. Just keeps disappearing. I don't understand why. Anyways let's see what happens if you increase the number here and here it should pretty much take the same amount of time if the speed doesn't have a cap on it. OK so he's like he has more opportunity to explore things. OK let's see how it all goes. And you can see the values are converging. They go up and down depending, you know, because there is some randomness and he might end up like in the pit even though he goes like this. But at the same time they're slowly starting to converge to some sort of values and cue values. OK, probably a thousand is a bit too much in terms of time. It doesn't look like the speed is proportionally increasing as well. So it might cut that part. I mean like reducing the speed. You know while this is very low you don't have to watch to the end of this project. I just want to experiment with quite a bit so as to give you some examples of what we've been working through but you get the point that it goes through all of this. It has some randomness like Rambler's built into his behavior. So even when it has a policy it will still continue exploring so it won't just like once it has a basic policy it won't just continue following its policy. It will still experiment with other variations once in a while in order to enhance its policy. Maybe it hasn't found the best policy already right away. Maybe it can improve the policy. And that's why even after so many iterations you can still see some random effects it is sometimes jumps in to random states not just because of the randomness in the environment but also because there is some level like a parameter which you could control which you could set up for your agent saying that's you know most of the time 80 percent of the time do whatever your policy tells you to do but 20 percent of the time you just have some fun experiment and see what happens and use that information that you gather to update your policy. OK this is taking way too long. Let's try that again. Yeah so that's how the agent learns in different states. Maybe let's just run one more just out of curiosity. So is there anything else we can change about it. Iterations. OK. OK let's have a look. Yeah well we could change the discussion for example. So in this case we could say K minus a hundred minus a Q minus two and minus are OK thousand. So reward. We want to keep it maybe let's keep it at 0.04 But let's say set against this keep the reward at my desert point zero for every time. And then here we're going to say that the discount is not zero point nine but it's like zero point point five. So it gets discounted quite a lot as you go through the game. So it actually now will be incentivized to be closer to the finish rather than further route. The states close to finish will get a high value so you can see that the value really drops off. It's not as green as it was before. So here you can see that this is the policy now. So it goes like that, like that , very similar to what we saw before, just probably only differences from here jumping straight into here. So that's one. And OK let's just run one more. This is so much fun. Let's just run one more so k minus k 100 a q discard. Keep it as it was original So let's just run this basic vanilla setup ok ok ok ok. It's going to see if it will show us the policy. And yes we got the policy. Yes. Good finish. So here we've got the policy. You know this is familiar. Remember that time when we saw that the AI outsmarted the human bomb into the wall to go there and boom into the wall to go like that to increase the problem. So there we go. That is an example of artificial intelligence inaction very very basic simple kill earnings so no deep learning at this stage. But at the same time it's already pretty smart and I hope you enjoyed today's project. And once again thank you to UC Berkeley and I hope you enjoyed today's project and I look forward to seeing them.

PLAN OF ATTACK

In today's section we're tackling the topic of deep Q learning. So let's see how we're going to attack this in this section. We will learn a deep learning intuition about the learning side of things so we separate deep learning from the intuition behind it into two parts: learning and acting. And we're going to have details on that. So first of all understand how the neural networks actually learn and how they update their weights based on what we are feeding them in and how the whole concept of learning works or how we're going to take the temporal difference concepts or re discuss and simple learning and apply them into deep learning and then we're going to talk about how deep learning algorithm actually decide what action to take in what states we're going to talk about experience replay a very important addition on top of deep learning which actually enables deep you'll learn to work properly and you'll see why it's important from that project. And then we're going to talk about action selection policies.

Plan of Attack

What we will learn in this section:

- Deep Q-Learning Intuition (Learning)
- Deep Q-Learning Intuition (Acting)
- Experience Replay
- Action Selection Policies

- Annex 1: Artificial Neural Networks

We're going to talk about how deep kill earning agents are able to combine exploration with exploitation. So once they find something a good approach they can use that approach but also they need to explore so that they don't get stuck in a local maximum. And one more thing I wanted to mention about the section is it is highly beneficial if you have a look at an x number one artificial neural networks. So if you go and explore all those topics we've got some very powerful intuition projects prepared for you there. If you haven't done, of course , if you haven't done the deep learning course, if you've done that, you plan of course and you already know all of these things and you can proceed with S.. But if you want to get that additional knowledge about neural networks before you proceed with this part of the course this is highly advisable because it will help you understand exactly how neural networks work and why they're so powerful and why we're leveraging them in this deep cool learning algorithm. And once you refresh your knowledge or gain that knowledge on neural networks from that annex and come back here and we will proceed with particularly if you're pretty comfortable in neural networks then let's get straight into it. Let's start talking about deep learning intuition. And I look forward to seeing the first project.

DEEP Q-LEARNING INTUITION

And finally we're on to the fun stuff we're onto deep learning. All right, so let's have a look. Bruce we spoke about killer earning and what it's all about. And we learned about the Agent environment and how the agent will look at the state. Or she is taking an action to get a reward. Enter into a new state and based on that feedback loop they will continue taking actions and they will learn from that. Understand what are the best actions to take. And so we looked at this basic example of a maze. We understood that as the Asian exploration environment understands what the values of the states are. Then we moved on from dealing with the values of the states to dealing with the values of the actions with the values and then A-Basin that we understood how plans in non sarcastic environments work and how policies work in stochastic environments and this is an example of a policy.

Deep Q-Learning Intuition

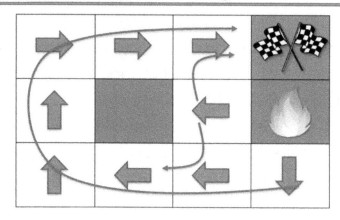

So that's a quick recap of everything we discussed in the basic learning. And now let's have a look at how this can be taken to the next level through deep learning through adding deep learning. OK. So this is our environment and what we're going to do now is we're going to add instead of just doing basic calculations in this matrix that we have which is pretty simple. What we're going to do is we're going to add two axes which add an x and y axis or we'll call them x1 and x2. Just to make things even more general. And here we've got the real number: the rows 1 2 three 4 he'll rule number the rows 1 to 3. And so now every single state can be described by a pair of two values x1 and x2 so any one of these squares in which the agent can possibly be in can be described by x1 x2. So for instance right now he's in the square with X1 equal to 1 and x 2 equal to 2. And therefore that's not some way we can escape in your square meaning we can describe in your state. Then of course this is a very simplified version of an environment describing States. But nevertheless it works in this case. And that means that now we can feed these states into a neural network. And by the way here I would just like to mention that at the end of the course of good annexes we've got an x number one and antics and two in order to proceed successfully with this section. Highly advisable that you check out unaccessible one which is on artificial neural network so you understand how they work so that we can we don't have to delve into that here and we can just use the benefits of the knowledge of how artificial neural networks work and so we feed this information on the state into a neural network and then it will process this information the X1 and x2 depending on the structure of the neural network it might have multiple hidden layers and so on. So that's something that you'll figure out in the practical projects but at the end we will structure in such a way that it spits out for values and these four values are actually going to be our Q value. So the values which dictate which action we need to take and the don't in this project will see exactly how these key values are used to decide which action is taken. But the main point here is that we no longer look at just this maze from a learning perspective. We're now taking the states of the maze and we're feeding them into a deep neural network in order to get these cubicles and. And at the end of the day we're still going to come up with an action we're still going to understand what action we need to take and we'll discuss all this in more detail but the question right now is why are we doing all of this why we called it.

Deep Q-Learning Intuition

Why are things so much more complicated when that initial approach of learning was working already well. The reason for that is that learning was working in this very simplistic environment and we're continuing to deal for now with this very simplistic environment in order to better understand the concepts. But at the same time that simple Kial learning will no longer work in more complex environments and we're talking about for instance the self-driving cars which will be creating or playing Doom when the artificial intelligence is playing Doom or other Atari games like breakout or even self-driving cars and more advanced reinforcement learning things such as like robots walking around and performing actions in all those cases basically learning is insufficient is not strong is not powerful enough to be able to master those challenges. And just like we've seen in the deep learning course if you've been in our discipline or if you've done the annex sections on x number one and X-2 you will know that deep learning is by far superior to any type of machine learning let alone a simple cool learning. And that's why we're leveraging the power of deep learning here so we're feeding in the information about the environment as a vector of values. In this case just to use into a deep neural network and then we're using that to perform the actions that we want to to decide which actions are agents going to take. So that's kind of like a high level overview of why we're doing this. And now let's have a look at in a bit more detail what happens to the concept of cool learning when we transfer when we make the transformation from or transition from simple learning into deep Killary. So as you saw in the previous intuition projects we had a slide like this which is the foundation of temporal difference learning. This is the formula for temporal difference and basically So let's go through. So basically we had an agent who was in this state over here which indicated the blue arrow. And we were understanding how temporal difference works for this value of for instance going up. And so what we saw here was before this is in the simple Killary not the deep learning is in the simple killer. What we saw was before the agent had a subsequent hue value that he had learned about this action of going up. And so then he decided to take ception to go up. And right after he takes his action he gets a reward for taking this action in this state. And that is the reward plus now he can evaluate the value of the current state he's in which is the maximum of all of the new q values of all of the cube of the new actions he can take a prime in the new state as print and read multiplied by the DK factor of gamma. So that is essentially the cue for the new cube value or kind of like the empirical cube value that he has just received for taking that action. And ideally these two two should be the same. So actually the Q value that he had in his memory about this action in this state should equate to the actual reward Plus the gamma times the value of the state that he ended up in. And therefore that's how we calculate the temporal difference. We take what you are after minus what he got, what he had in mind, what he was expecting. You'd subtract one from the other. That's a temporal difference. And then you use your learning rate Alpha to adjust your q value to your new q value by the temporal difference but with a coefficient of Alpha. So that is the essence of simple learning. Now let's have a look at how it changes in deep Killary and so we are still going to work with the slide but we're going to just see exactly what's happening. So in deep learning the neural network will predict for Valis as we saw in the previous and as we'll see. Donna Citronelle the neural network will predict for values or it might predict more values of more possible actions in a given state. But in this case we know that there's only four upright actions left to be done. And so the neural network will predict four of these values so there will be no end in a deep learning situation. It is important that there is no before or after. And this is how we'll get to know this a bit better. So the neural network will predict four of these values and it will compare not to what will happen after but the neural network will compare to this exact value but it was the value which was calculated in the previous step. So in the previous time when the agent was in this exact square. So let's say I don't know some time ago the agent was again in this exact square as well and it calculated this value previously. So in the previous time a long time ago the agent calculated this value then the agents stored this value for the future and now the future has come. So now he's in the square again and now he's got these cube values which are predicted and one of them is for the four going up. So now what he's going to do is to compare the predicted value of Q to this value which he had recorded from the previous step and will understand exactly why this is important right now, so just important to understand here. There's no before an officer in this specific square this specific time.

Deep Q-Learning Intuition

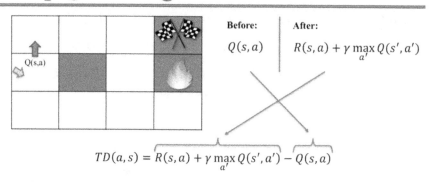

$$TD(a, s) = R(s, a) + \gamma \max_{a'} Q(s', a') - Q(s, a)$$

We're taking the Q value that he's predicted using the neural network this time and we comparing it to this value which he had from the previous time from the previous time he was in this square assessing all of the situation and you know like the previous time he actually performed this action. So there we go. Now let's have a look at how this all works out in the neural network and why. Why is it like I know it sounds a bit complicated right now but we'll break it down into simple terms just in a second. So this on your own network we're feeding in the states of the environment into the neural network is going through the hidden layers that it's coming out with these outputs Q1 Q2 Q3 Q4. In that specific state these are the cube values that the neural network is predicting for possible actions. Those are cumulous. So then we're appearing to target and these targets exist exactly so if we go back here this is the target so this is the value that was predicted. And then we also know that we have a target from the last time we were in the square. We have a target for this same action which is up for instance. So here we've got a target and we're going to compare we're comparing Q1 versus that target we're comparing Q2 versus that target the target that we had from previously Q3 versus a target Q4 versus the target. And so this is the part where the neural network or the agent is now learning through deep learning how to better go through. And the key point here is that we're still applying cool learning but the concept's answer is simple : you learn through temporal differences which are pretty straightforward which we've already discussed and we know quite well why not. But at the same time in deep learning how do neural networks learn through adjusting the weights. So we have to adapt the concepts of reinforcement, the concepts of simple kill learning, to the way neural networks actually work. And that is through updating their weights. And so this is what we're trying to figure out here: how do we adapt that concept of temporal difference to our own network so that we can leverage the full power of neural networks. So far we've gotten this so we enter our environment state here as a vector goes through a neural network we get predictions of key values and then from the previous time the agent was in that state. We have these new targets to target

one, two , three and four for each of these respective
actions. And so now we're up to it. OK let's compare each
one with each one. And from here it becomes pretty
straightforward if you're up to speed with neural
networks. Once again that's on an Anax.

Deep Q-Learning Intuition

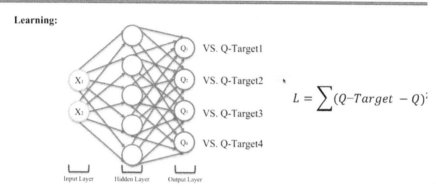

Number one we're going to calculate a loss which is here
and we're going to target this one minus A minus this
one. We're going to square that so the square difference
of each one of these and we're going to sum them. So we
take the sum of the squared differences of these values
and their targets and we're going to send them up and
that's going to be a loss. And so ideally just as we had into
in the temporal difference learning so if we go back for a
second remember we said Ideally we want this to be

119

equal to this so we want the temporal difference to be zero so that's that means basically the agent is predicting exactly correctly what you know the Q value is that the agent is predicting are exactly or that he has and memory are exactly descriptive of the environment and therefore the agent can never get the environed pretty well right.

Deep Q-Learning Intuition

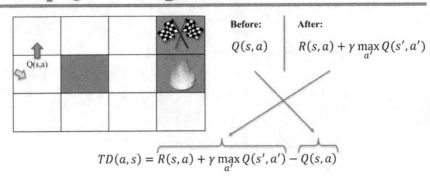

$$TD(a, s) = R(s, a) + \gamma \max_{a'} Q(s', a') - Q(s, a)$$

There's no surprises there's no there's no s.a as long as a temporal difference is a pilot highly positive or highly negative. Then we've got some surprises. But if the general differences are zero then he knows the environment so well that he can predict what's going on and he can and therefore his policy is going to be very good and he's going to be able to navigate. So here. Same thing so we want this law to be as close to zero I suppose as smallest possible. And that's why now we're going to this is the part where we are going to leverage the real true power of neural network so we're going to take this loss and we're going to use back propagation or stick as the gradient descent to take this loss and pass it through the network posit back or back propagated through a network and through to cast a great and decent a date the weights. All of these synapses in the network so that next time we go through this network the way it's already a bit better descriptive of the environment and that's exactly what we're. So here you have if you go back this is calculated losses Kalka and guess prove propagator for the network the weights are updated. Then the next time we get here this happens again and again here this happens again and so on and so and it keeps happening and that's how this agent learns or basically now the neural network which is the brain of the agent is learning is becoming more and more descriptive of the environment and therefore the agent is able to navigate the environment. When we say descriptive environment basically means that when we put in the states of the environment that this agent is in we are more likely to get closer and closer to the actual cue values and that happens because the cube values that we want to find the right action and that happens because these new targets are actually empirically derived so he every day how does he find these cute targets. That's actually there so he actually observes. OK so once I do take this step what's the reward I get. And then what's the values of this state? So the same thing as we saw previously in Q learning and the simple learning intuition. So he learns this through trial and error and then he constructs his network or that's the way it is in such a way that the predicted values are close and close. Consummating that target. Q values are very similar to the concept we discussed here in the simple temporal difference learning of the simple skill learning algorithm. So there you go.

DEEP Q-LEARNING INTUITION – ACTING

The previous part we talked about the deep learning Killary intuition we started there. And in fact we actually got all the way to this part and where we talked about learning and now we're going to move on to the actual acting part. So there's two distinct parts that we have to remember. So that's the learning part but now he actually he's done all of this. That's beautiful. Now he actually has to take action. He has to decide what he is going to do is going to do action one, two , three or four. And so how does he do that? Well the way he does it is now given those same values so the values don't change after we've had these values or compare them with Calcott the last two. By the arrogant era we've updated the weights but the values don't change in that whole process. To have got the cube values there. They're fixed. We know what they are. All this happens though. Networks updated and out using those same values that we had. What we're going to do is we're going to parse them through a soft max function. And again soft Max as described. I think annex 2 and we'll talk a bit more about soft max. Further down in or we'll talk about this action selection policy further down in the rest of this section. So just in a few projects. But for now we're just going to say we're passing it through a soft next function.

Deep Q-Learning Intuition

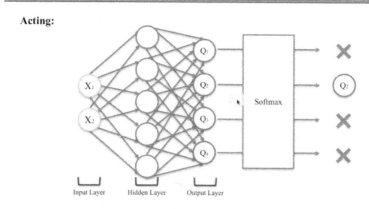

Acting:

Basically what it does is it allows it to select the best one and it selects the best action possible. And there's a small caveat to that. It's not just the best one possible. We'll talk about that in the action selection policy project. But for now let's just say it selects the best action from here it says OK so Q1 you know the likelihood. Basically we know that q values predict the Q value so it can look at them and say OK so the highest Q value of these just as we did in the simple Q learning algorithm. I'll just look at all these to say the highest values, this one I'm going to select that action we're going to take. And that's pretty much it. That's how he chooses which action to take , takes action and then all of this process happens again. For the next stage the agent ends up in our case and the next square of the maze. But generally speaking in the next state. So there we go. That's how we feed in a reinforcement learning problem into a neural network through a vector describing the state that we're in. And once we fit it. There's two parts of the process that happen. Part one is the learning. So remember that part where we compare each of the cube values with the target and then we back propagate the loss through the network to update the weights so that our network is learning as we go through this maze or through this environment. And also the second part is of course we have to act we have to select an action and that is where we pass the values through a soft max function and or basically an action selection policy which we'll talk about further down. And then we simply select the action that we want to take and we perform that action and then this whole process starts again. And then maybe the agent gets then maybe the agent doesn't pause the game. In any case the game ends. And then once again the whole process repeats.

The agent plays the whole game again and then that stops so basically that's another airpark every time the agent you know every time the game ends with a favor beyond fairie that's the end of an airport. And then he starts again and then he starts again and then he starts again. And so on.

Deep Q-Learning Intuition

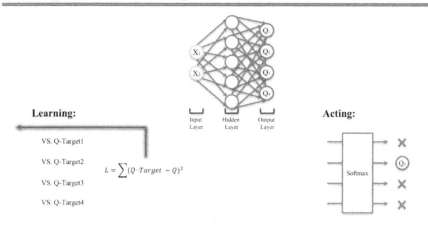

So that happens and this process happens for every single time the agent is in you in a new state so the state is encoded here so that's important not just for every single game that he plays but for every single state. So he's in a state that goes through his process dates and so on and happens every single time. And so the learning happens and the acting happens as well. So that is deep learning in the intuition behind deep learning. We've got lots more to cover off and then of course practical and in the meantime if you'd like to get some additional information on keep learning. We've got a recommended reading so we've already spoken about Arthur Giuliani's series of blog posts. If you look at simple informal learning of Lifton's flow part 4 you will find the part that's relevant to what we discussed today. Note that here he talks about convolutions. We are not covering revolutions in this section; we're going to be talking about them in the next section of the course. So the difference here is that it's just kind of skip the conclusions part for now and we'll talk about them in the next part of the course but the difference is in evolutions. You're like the agent is looking at the image and therefore he has to process an image, an additional complication for now where we're slowly gradually building up to that. For now we're encoding our environment through you look here we're encoding our environment or maybe look at this one probably in coding our environment as a or in to state the agent is in as a vector. So in our case it was a very simple vector of values. Sometimes people even in that simple may sometimes or as you'll see from this blog post. Sometimes people prefer the one hot and coded version of that state. So basically where every single box of the maze has a. So you have like a vector of for a null case would be 12 values three by four. So it isn't like either 1 or 0 depending on which elements and which box you're in. In the environment. So in whichever way you decide to code your environment and the state of your environment that's how in coding It's basically a vector. The key here is that it's not a convolution So it's not like an image and there's no convolution volt So this part will come later. For us it starts over here and that just simplifies the process for us to gradually understand better. And of course don't forget that this post is rude and tends to flow and we're using pi torche in our projects. So hopefully you enjoy this. A quick intro into a deep convolutional deep not yet deep book learning. And on that note I look forward to seeing you next.

EXPERIENCE REPLAY

All right so I hope you're enjoying the project so far we're nearly done with the intuition you will soon very soon get to the practical side of things. We've just got a few little things that we need to cover. All right so previously we talked about how we add neural networks into this whole equation of CULE learning and take ular into the next step and turn it into deep learning. And today we're going to add an extra important feature which will be coding in the practical side of things, so I decided that it's important for us to cover it often in the intuition side of things so that you're more prepared for it when it comes to the coding side of things. So as we discussed we've got the network there's two parts that happen. First of all it's the learning so the network actually learns with every new state it. It slowly updates its waits to get better and better and better at dealing with this environment. And then there is the acting inside the state so after the q values have been counted in the state then once you select.

Experience Replay

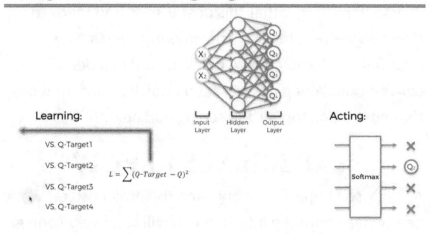

$$L = \sum (Q\text{-}Target - Q)^2$$

Learning:

VS. Q-Target1

VS. Q-Target2

VS. Q-Target3

VS. Q-Target4

Input Layer Hidden Layer Output Layer

Acting:

Softmax

So today we're still going to talk about the learning part we're going to come up with an interesting feature that's going to help in undergrad to come up with this feature ourselves but we'll talk about a feature that is very important for deep , cool learning and that feature is called experience replay. All right. So here is our network so we've just copied it over here. We've got that lost Calcott at the bottom is a back propagator through the network. And let's have a look at an example of what happens to understand the problem that we're dealing with a bit better. So here is an example actually from the scores. This is a screen shot shot exactly from this course. This is what you will be programming. This is a self-driving car that is driving through this road and it has to learn how to navigate this road. And so what it is as we discussed previously What is this in this state. And of course the state is not going to be x1 x2 Lundell just describe it in a lot more detail what the state is, it is going to be a couple of parameters which relate to the angle of the car and some relative parameters that the sensors are reading and so on. So there's going to be more parameters than that to describe the state. But nevertheless it's going to be a vector of values going through a neural network and then on the output you're going to have some ACU values. Again there'll be a difference depending on the environment. There can be a different number of possible actions. But we're just going to for simplicity sake leave it at for just for us to be able to understand better what's going on here. So in this case what is the question is so far what is this. This inputs into this neural network or more specifically how often do we trigger this neural net. How often does this neural net grow? Well every time the car ends up in a new state so the car makes a move it ends up in a new state and then everything goes. All that data, all that information from about the state goes through the network gives Alice the calculated errors. This error is calculated based on what we discussed in previous projects. This is back propagated through and their weights are updated. Then the car selects which action was to take and makes that move and ends up in a new state in the new state. Everything starts over again. And so basically this happens every time the car is in and you said well have a look at this example. I specifically took the screenshot because it looks very well illustrates the problem that is addressed through experience replay and expense replays, not just something that we use in this course or in this specific problem. It is something that you will see used throughout. On and on and over and over again in artificial intelligence algorithms because it is so powerful and it's so important. So look at this car, this car in this problem or in this environment. Its goal is to come from here to here and back. Its goal is to navigate its way here without crossing these walls which are made of sand. And so the car started over here it went down and like its reward is based on you know how close it is to start. So the car went from here it went down and kept going like this or along this wall along the seawall. And what is it going to do next is going to turn is going to keep going. Well what we wanted to do is keep going here. But let's think about it for a second. Once it gets to this wall every single time it moves forward it moves forward. It moves forward it moves forward moves forward moves forward moves forward and so on it moves forward. So depending on the structure, the environment could be like a hundred moves here or 50 moves here. It just keeps moving forward forward forward forward for it and

130

nothing changes. Not really changes it gets way further away from this started closer to this story. That's lovely. But in terms of the surrounding environment not many things are changing it's still that same wall. If you are sitting in the car you probably see the situation when you're driving in whatever you're seeing is like the environment is so monotonous that you're just seeing kind of the same thing just passing by. But like I imagine you're driving through a desert and you're just seeing the same thing it's the same sound it's the same sound nothing is happening. Nothing is changing. And so based but every single time we're putting that new state into here. Yes of course something might be changing for us as you're driving the car and your GPS is showing you're closer to your destination. So one of these inputs is strange but a lot of these other inputs the sensors for instance which are on the car they're not changing and therefore as you're driving slow in this day to put in put the inputs into your own into here and all the time the inputs are pretty much the same. And so if you keep inputting the same inputs with the same values in vectors or very similar vectors into your network because there is no variety. The car will learn very well. One thing you'll learn very well is how to drive along this wall which is on its right and so that's how the network will update and it will slowly start getting rewarded for driving so well it will be like. OK so up from here I'll be learning all I'm doing so good I'm doing better I'm doing it better. That's all. It will have this false perception that it's actually doing very well even though it only learns how to drive along as well as other neural networks will become very adapted to driving along this well and then all of a sudden there's this curve and the car doesn't know what to do. And it completely doesn't fit in with this neural network. And even if it does it just somehow let's hypothetically say passes a spot and then it ends up on this wall. Same thing is going to happen from here to here. OK now the neural network is restructuring itself to adapt to this wall and then bam this thing happens. And then even if somehow it gets passed that it will drive past this thing and then the same thing along these lines. So basically this is a very vivid example of the problem that we are what we have is that because the way we're using the neural net updating it every single state once we have lots of consecutive stuff they don't even have to be the same but there is in environments that's normal that is consecutive states are somehow correlated or are somehow interdependent and we don't want that interdependency to bias our network. We don't want the car to just learn how to drive along like a straight line or a long curved line or like anything that you think that you can think of in in life where an agent would be Navigant environment where we can think of correlated or interdependent states that come after another that can really mess up your neural network. If you are just going to let the agent learn from that. And that's where experience replay comes in. What happens in experience replay is these experiences so these states that it's in one two three however many 50 states here in neuro they don't get put through the network right away. They are actually saved into memory of the agent. And so for instance it saves all these and saves all these and some at some point once it reaches a certain threshold which you'll be able to code and Atlanta will show you how to do that. Once it reaches a certain threshold then the agent decides for itself OK it's time to learn. I have this batch of experiences that I have. I'm not going to learn from that and so randomly selecting a uniform distribution and uniformity is key here because that's something we'll talk about on the next slide. We'll mention that. But it takes a uniformly distributed sample. So basically all experiences are considered to be equal. It takes a uniformly distributed sample from that batch of experiences that it has and then it goes through them and learns from them so it doesn't take all the experience or just takes it uniformly distribute samples it might take couple of from here a couple from here a couple from here and it and each experience is characterized by the state it was in the action that it took the state it ended up in and the reward it it achieved through that action in that specific state so four elements in each experience state one action state two and reward and so it takes all those experiences and then it passes them through the network and it learns. And that way it breaks the pattern of that bias which comes from the sequential nature of the experience as if you were to put them through the network one after the other. So that's the main focus of the experience we play. That's what the problem and address is and another benefit of experience replay is that sometimes in an environment like this you might have very valuable rare experiences. So for instance I don't know let's say let's look at this corner right this is this is the right corner. Right. And a very sharp one is sharp. So it'll be coming from here assuming it's going to be hugging this corner. So having you sharp right corners we have in this whole we're going to have one right corner here and one right corner here. Right so when it's coming this way that's the right corner. And then when it's going back it's a sharp right corner here. And this one's not sharp this way in the shop so there's only one opportunity in the whole environment to learn from a sharp right corner. And that's a very important experience because you might get really good at driving along straight lines and get really good at doing soft corners like that. And then it'll keep messing up this sharp right corner simply because it doesn't have that much opportunity to learn from it and so therefore it will learn everything else very quickly but it'll take a long time to learn the right course. It's a very simplified example of a very simplified explanation but it illustrates the concept that sometimes they are rare experiences which can be valuable. And if you're just doing a simple neural network where you're putting in your values here and you know they're going through and you know like even if you forget about that problem of the sequential nature of experiences and how they can be interdependent and all correlated Thimphu even forget about that for a second. What happens is once you put an experience in it goes through networks up data then you instantly forget but forget about that experience. You move on to the next one. That's just how the neural network works. Then you move onto the next state, the next step, the next step, the next experience AND experience that experience and so on. So this right corner as soon as it goes through a network is gone and you don't have any memory of that valuable experience. Whereas we've experienced replay because you're putting these experiences into batches you can organize your bash as a rolling window so for instance you could have like 100 batches So hundred experiences in your batch so when it's coming back from here it's as soon as it has recorded this experience in its batch. Then like at some point it runs it takes a uniform distribution from its batch of experiences and then there's a rolling window so it forgets these experiences but then it keeps these experiences. And then again it learns from once it's here it learns from this batch and then once it's here it forgets all the way up to here. But then it has a batch of experiences like that so therefore not learn from these experiences. And that way what you are getting is that this right hand corner might come up several times in its learning process because it was in that batch when the batch was like this around there than there was in the batch here in about here so it came up in several batches because the abash might be updated as a rolling window of experience.

Experience Replay

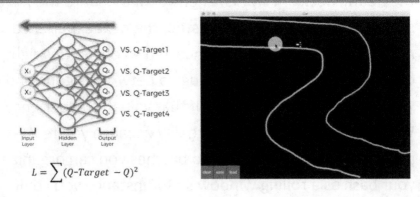

$$L = \sum (Q\text{-}Target - Q)^2$$

So the older experiences get kicked out, the newer experiences are added and then again older experiences get it. So an experience stays in the batch for quite some time and the car or agent can learn from that experience several times. So that's another advantage of experience replay. And of course the final advantage is experience replay gives you an opportunity to learn from more experiences than if you're just learning for one at a time because you have that batch and therefore it's a rolling window and therefore even if your environment is limited to experience your experience replay approach can help you learn faster. And instead of just redoing it there are many many many times you can learn fast because you don't have to redo it. You have those experiences saved. So those are the main advantages of experience. Let's recap what we've got. We're breaking that pattern over independence and correlation of sequential experiences. We save rare experiences which might be important therefore we can learn from them more often and we can learn in environments we can learn Fosler environments which are experiences. We have a shortage of experiences which don't have that many experiences that the agent goes through and still we can be able to learn that. So that is what experience replays all about. If you'd like to read a bit more than this. There's an interesting article published by deep mind in 2016 called prioritized experience replay and it talks about why. Why are we using a uniform distribution to select our experiences from the experience of Bachche ? Why don't we find a better way to select our experiences and prioritize some of the experiences which we feel that are important. It's quite an interesting thing though in this case you will be able to not only reinforce or not only reinforce your knowledge on experience replay but you will actually be able to move with the cutting edge of technology.

Additional Reading

Additional Reading:

Prioritized Experience Replay

Tom Schaul et al.,
Google DeepMind (2016)

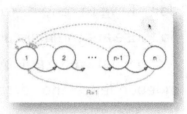

Link:

https://arxiv.org/pdf/1511.05952.pdf

So this is 2016 and published by deep minds. It's a very recent very powerful paper so you'll be able to actually explore the limits or explore even further this algorithm and take it to the next level. So I'll leave it up to you to find out why and how we can change the uniform to a different approach to experience replay from this paper if you'd like. And I hope you enjoy this. Tauriel and now we know what experience really is and we can confidently use it in our practical circles and I look forward to seeing you next time.

ACTION SELECTION POLICIES

I hope you're enjoying the course so far. And today we're talking about action selection policies. All right let's get straight into it. Previously we talked about adding a neural network to our simple learning and so far we are getting quite into deep learning. We've talked about the learning part quite a bit including adding some elements to it. And today we're talking about this part we're talking about the acting. So let's have a look. So here we've got what we discussed about acting: once you input the values the parameters are the vector describing the state agent clearly in that environment then that is after all the learning is done or even before the learning is done. Basically we get all the q values so we're not interested in the learning right now we insist on acting so once we have these key values how do we understand which one we need to use. Well if you think about it. Q values are simply predictions for the cube. So as we did in the simple learning algorithm what did we do we just selected the one with the best of the highest value. Once we have the one with the highest IQ value we just take that action because it just brings us the highest value and that we know that Duval's calculator's immediate reward that we expect to receive Plus the DK factor times the value of the next date. And it's a recursive calculation so why not why wouldn't you take the best value and that's kind of the end of it. But as you can see here it's not as simple here we're using a soft max function and this is where we're going to talk about actual selection policies. So here in reality we don't have to have just a software function. We can have different action selection policies for example we've got Epsilon greedy Epsilon's soft and we've got the soft Macs and those are kind of like the most commonly used action selection policies of course there are others. For instance the most basic one is a very simple action, it just selects the best. The one with the highest Q value. But why doesn't that action pulse fly and why do we have different types of action pulse action selection policies. Well it all boils down to exploration versus exploitation. And that is the core of reinforcement learning because we already talked about this a little bit that your agent when it's operating in an environment it might predict certain queue values which might be good and it might turn out great it might turn out that those are available and will be forced to explore. So if we for instance in this case predict that Q2 is the best one and then it takes Q To take action to and it. So from here to Section 2 and then it gets a very negative reward. Then the environment is forcing the agent to go and explode because now he's going to learn that oh actually I thought Q2 was going to be very good but it turned out very bad. So the results are not very bad. So the network can update itself so next time he's in the state he's going to probably eat my soul just to get it. You know, like if it is very very favorable so you might think that that's like you know you might need a couple of times a couple of penalties or punishments in order to learn it is about action. But maybe he'll already soon learn that I'm going to take a different action and take the wrist action because now it has the best value. So sometimes the environment forces the agent to take different actions to explore different actions but sometimes the agent might find itself stuck in a local maximum. It might find that it followed through its initial exploration and found that oh this is a pretty cool action like I'm going to go right here. And that d'esprit collection. But the problem is that it thinks is the best action simply because it hasn't explored is explored going up his nose or going left is explore going right but it hasn't explored going down from that specific state that it's in and now that it's kind of like biased towards this action and think thinks a good action is going to keep taking it is going to keep getting. He's going to keep talking and is actually going to keep getting a good reward. But what if this action would have been even better if this action would have been so much better that if it knew about this action it would actually switch to this action but because it got stuck in a local maximum it is just going to be reinforced. This is going to keep reinforcing itself or the violence going to reinforce it that this is a good action to take and keep doing that. But really the reality is that there's this other action that hasn't been found yet or hasn't even been explored. That would have been much better. So what we want to do is we want to come up with an actual selection policy that allows our agent not to get stuck in a local maximum. Yes it's important to you know keep doing the good actions that's the exploitation part. We won't exploit what we've found. But at the same time we still want to explore. We never want to stop exploring as in life you never want to stop learning you stop learning you die. That's things like that when you're not growing you're dying or something got so you want to keep learning and your agent wants to keep learning. And that's where these action selection policies come in. So we've got three you listed here so the first one is Epsilon greedy. It's a very simple one. It sounds pretty complex in the sense that it's got a cool name and usually things with surgical names. It's actually not. So basically what it does is it will select the one with the best Q value and epsilon like Epsilon you might hear other places it's just like a selection policy. So in this case we're using it to slick so our out of AI-Q values are by sales like the one with the highest Q value all the time except for Epsilon percent of the time. So for instance if you set epsilon to 10 percent then you're going to or 0.1 than 10 percent of the time that the action is going to be selected at random. So 90 percent of the time you're still going to be selecting the best action based on the highest value. But 10 percent of the time is going to be selecting a random action. Uniform it is going to be absolutely randomly taking an action or if you said epsilon to zero point five for 0.05 that means that 95 percent of the time the agent is going to be taking the action with the highest value. But 5 percent of the time it's still going to be selecting and random action. So it's going to be going out there and exploring. So Epsilon's software is very similar to the way that it does kind of like why it's called FCL greedy because then you're greedily selecting the good action except for that little episode. Some of the time. So the lower the EPS deal they'll lower the Lepp Epsilon the more greasily you're selecting that kind of the action that is the optimal action and the less you're leaving the less chances you leave for exploration Epsilon's soft is the opposite. So basically you're selecting at random you're selecting one minus Epsilon cent of the time. So if you epsilons like 0.1 to 10 percent then only 10 percent of the time you're taking this action. And 90 percent of the time you're selecting a random action. So very very simple just inverted algorithms and a soft Max is kind of like the next step from or it's a more advanced version I would say over epsilon or epsilon greedy algorithm although they both have merit and they both have a place.

Action Selection Policies

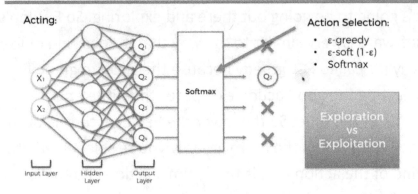

Acting:

Q_1 Q_2 Q_3 Q_4

X_1 X_2

Softmax

Q_2

Input Layer   Hidden Layer   Output Layer

Action Selection:

- ε-greedy
- ε-soft (1-ε)
- Softmax

Exploration
vs
Exploitation

We're going to be using self-finance in our coding in our practical sort of thing. So that's what we're going to talk about in a bit more detail about soft max. So let's have a look. So let's move on to your next hopefully. It's pretty clear that Ebsen agrees it's a pretty straightforward algorithm. Select this one. Most of the time except for sometimes going and exploring. And now we also see why it's important to do that exploration so that we don't end up in local maximums in our optimization process so now we're going to talk a bit more about soft Macs. There's a project on soft marks at the end of the course. I think it's annex number two where we talk about the concept of Maxim's because you refresh a little bit here so there we're talking about neural networks and by the way we're all going to be covering convolutional. We're not covering evolution neural networks in this section. Of course in this section we're still using a vector. But in the next section of the course when we're we're creating an AI to play Doom we are going to be using convolutional neural network so it could be beneficial for you to look at in relational neural networks and then take a self max function or you can learn a bit more about soft Max. After you take the convolutional neural networks and of course later on. But here's a quick refresher So here we've got our convolutional neural network which decides whether it's a dog or cat. So here we've got the voting process between these neurons and this one says that it's a it's got the features you know the fluffy ears What's the pointed pointed face type of thing and the kind of the features are the types of eyes the eye with eyes look all these features that belong to a dog. So there's a 95 percent chance that it's a dog and a 5 percent chance that it's a cat. But the question is how did we get in that Tauriel we're talking about how do we get these values to add up to one.

Action Selection Policies

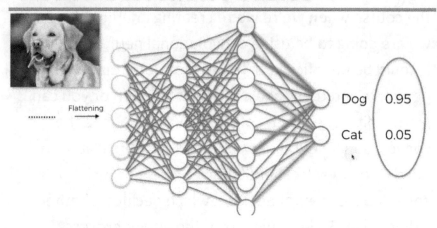

Well whatever convolutional all our whole neural
networks are the convolutional neural network plus the
fully connected Lares whatever it's bad out whatever the
values that we apply to soft max function are here. This is
where we introduced the formula for the soft next
function. Is what it looks like. And then we got these
values. And so basically that's a quick refresher.

Action Selection Policies

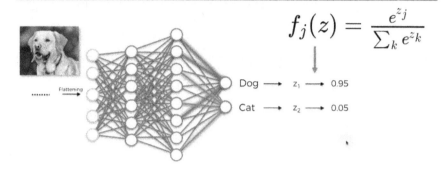

$$f_j(z) = \frac{e^{z_j}}{\sum_k e^{z_k}}$$

Dog $\longrightarrow$ z_1 $\longrightarrow$ 0.95

Cat $\longrightarrow$ z_2 $\longrightarrow$ 0.05

This is the formula for the soft Max. It's what it does is it takes however many outputs you have doesn't matter. It will take them and it will squash them all into values between 0 and 1 regardless of how big they are. Just because it's for me you can see that there's a total sum at the bottom so these devices are going to be zero and in. And also all these values are going to add up to one always. And so that's very beneficial for us because when we're using the soft max function what happens is we get these values and we select the best view value. But in reality what happens is these values that we get there are actual numbers right. So these are some kind of numbers. They don't have to all add up to one and don't have to be between 0 and 1. Just some numbers. But when we apply soft Max we don't just select the best one we actually get numbers like that so we get our numbers in the range between 0 and 1 and that are also that also add up to 1. And so what other thing do we know that adds up to one. Well probabilities we know that probabilities always have to add up to 1 so that is why we can say here we've got q values but here all of a sudden we've got soft or we've got probabilities. So we can say that the likelihood of this being the best action is 90 percent. This lesbian section 5 percent 2 percent 3 percent because we know the higher your value the better the action. So if we squash them to 0 to 1 then these become possibilities and we can deal with them as such. And therefore now is when the action is selected and that's how we come up with Q2. But if you look at it closely this isn't a strict 100 percent and these are not Saroo 0 percent. So this is 5 percent to 3 percent. So the most natural way to apply the soft Max in order to preserve exploration in the algorithm is to use these exact probabilities as how often we're going to be taking that action. So these probabilities actually present the distribution of these actions that we're taking so basically soft Max makes it very easy for us to come up with a way to combine exploitation and exploration. So the best the best action will always have the high probability because it has highest Q value and therefore here we're going to be just going to use these as our distribution or we're going to say okay we're going to be taking Q2 90 percent of the time but 5 percent of the time we still get to be taking Q1 and 2 percent of the time we get to 3 and 3 percent of the time we're going to be taking Q4. And the beauty here is also that as these values update as and as the agent goes through the network more and more and more it becomes more familiar with with the environment and therefore these updates so this value for instance might become like it might might ascertain that this value is actually less or this actually is higher and so these probabilities will also change as an agent goes through. So even though here we've got Choo-Choo. Nobody is to say that sometimes 5 percent of the time to be more precise we'll be selecting Q1 as the action to take and sometimes or action one will be taking action one. Sometimes will be taking action through a two action three two percent of the time and action for will be taking about 3 percent. So every action has a chance to play in this process as long as we have enough iterations an agent goes through lots and lots of times through these states that they're in. And that's how this that's how any kind of deep learning algorithm works that you want to do this many many times so that you learn from experience and therefore as you can see here it's a very natural transition to. We're not just randomly like an Epson angry algorithm and not just randomly selecting the actions we're selecting them based on their soft max values which makes it makes it like has some logic behind it not just not just that random 10 percent of the time we're selecting a random action but there's some logic behind how we're doing it and based on the key values that we've explored.

Action Selection Policies

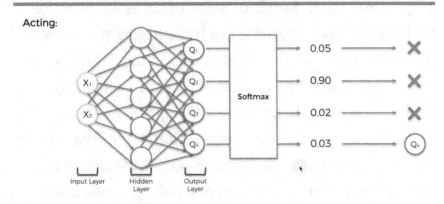

Acting:

Input Layer   Hidden Layer   Output Layer

And so that's the action selection policy that we're going to be using in this course. You're welcome to definitely check out Ebsen greedy action section Polsce if you like but we're going to be predominately using the soft Max action selection policy and I've got an interesting reading for you. So this is called adaptive Epsilon greedy exploration in reinforcement learning based on value differences. It's the 2010 article. And it's interesting because Mike Michel I'm not sure how to pronounce Michelle and Miquel toxic introduces a different type of Algren's and adjusted Epsilon greedy algorithm and called the VDB VDB algorithm or epsilon greedy VDB algorithm you can see here. And he actually compares it to the Ebsen greedy and soft Max and it's an absolute greedy algorithm which basically the main idea behind it is to adjust the value of epsilon depending on the state the agent is in. So if the agent is very certain about the state then Epsilon should be smaller so there should be less exploration if the agent is answered Epson's should be higher should be more exploration. So it is a 2010 article. I'm not sure if it's if this new proposed algorithm is widely used or is being accepted in the community or if artificial Times has kind of a way from this suggestion.

Additional Reading

Additional Reading:

Adaptive ε-greedy Exploration in Reinforcement Learning Based on Value Differences

Michel Tokic (2010)

Link:

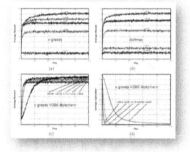

http://tokic.com/www/tokicm/publikationen/papers/AdaptiveEpsilo nGreedyExploration.pdf

But nevertheless it will definitely help you reinforce your knowledge about action selection policies which we discussed the Epsom Ingredion the soft Naxal help you i'll give you an opportunity to compel Subha site and also see in which direction people actually think when they want to improve artificial intelligence so if you're ever planning on creating really interesting algorithms that are pushing the edge of Elche artificial intelligence and pushing the envelope in this space then this could be a good way for you to see in which direction people think sometimes when they're trying to improve the norms of artificial intelligence or the norms that existed back then in 2010. So there we go. Hopefully you enjoyed today's project about the action selection policies and we learned about abseil greedy Epsom salt and the soft Macs and now you're even more prepared for the practical side of things. And on that note I look forward to seeing your next step.

WINDOWS OPTION 2 - PART A INSTALLING UBUNTU ON WINDOWS

This is Carol or Manco and today we're going to be installing Linux onto our machines and right away. Apologies for my voice. I lost my voice over the past week and it's coming back slowly but not fully yet but I hope it will be ok today. So there isn't always the Tauriel that pie towards it doesn't actually work on Windows it only works on Linux or Mac. So if you have a Mac you definitely are fine you don't even need to do this project at all. On the other hand if you have windows you need to install a virtual machine and then on top of that virtual machine you were going to install Linux and then into that Linux that's where we're going to install Anaconda. By then by torching everything and we're going to be doing all of our work inside a virtual machine simply because that's the only way we can get a pite torch to run. So that's what we're going to be doing in the store. And I'm going to quickly show you a demonstration of what we're working towards. This is a virtual box manager where the virtual machines are stored and will create one of these. And this is me running a virtual machine right now so you can see that this is like a computer inside a computer is a virtual environment here and give it a second so you can see now. It's slowly loading. All right there we go. So this is Linux. To be specific Kubuntu inside my windows. And now here I can install an icon in the Python by torch and everything and do my work here. So that's what we're working towards. Let's get rid of this and let's create our own virtual machine. All right. So first things first.

We're going to start with an article we're going to be following the instructions in this article. So go to instruct if you need to bring this up on your own if you follow these. Go to Instructables dot com slash I.D. slash introduction dash. Thirty eight says Windows 7 but this should be fine for Windows 10 as well. OK. So the first thing we want to do is we won't install the virtual box and you can get it here at Virtual Box dot org. And if it's free it's absolutely free. So just click here and it all downloads. You need this one virtual box. Whatever version budgeted for Windows hosts You could also do that on Linux as well but on Mac. But really you don't need to because Pitre runs fine on Mac. So once it's downloaded it just goes through the installation and as it says here just keep all the defaults, continue all of the defaults and once you're done you'll get a virtual box on your computer or something like this. So let's quickly open it up. Just to show you there is Ron and then you just go like I already have, offering to repair the virtual box but you should just install it. It's a very straightforward process. All right so once you've installed virtual box now is when we can create our virtual machines. So again we're going to be following these instructions. I'm just going to walk through it instead of like reading it reading the instructions but if he ever so up to this point if he ever really likes to get lost you can always refer to these instructions as well. All right, so let's have a look.

I will create a new virtual machine. Let's call it a box here. Make sure to select Linux and then you need a boon to 64

155

bit click next year to add some memory. This is the RAM memory which is which you can change later on. So it's no big deal if you know you set it too low or too high right now. And do you find that your you know programs are not working as quickly as you'd like to. You can always adjust later on. I'll show you how. But for now you know I just said it somewhere wherever you like somewhere I said somewhere in the middle create a virtual Virtual Hard Disk now. Yes you want to create a virtual hard disk. And bear in mind this hardest that you're going to create is going to go onto your main harddrive. So on the one where your Windows is installed that's where it is going to go. So make sure you have enough space there and we'll talk about space in seconds so VDI is what we need dynamically allocated means that the amount of space on your hard drive is allocated as is required. You can choose either I choose dynamically allocated so click next adds here I like 10 gigabytes is not enough. You should have more than that you should allocate about right now, allocating about 50 to that previous Virtual Box. And it's dynamically allocated. If you choose that option it should be like any big problem but just make sure you have enough space on your hard drive so 10 gigabytes is definitely not enough. You need a bit more than that.

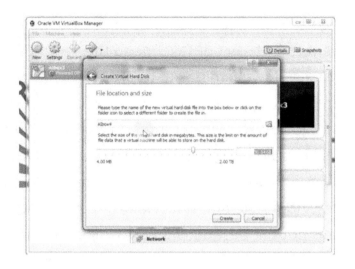

So click Create and there you go. So there is your virtual box that's all created. It doesn't have Linux on it though. If you still need to install Linux. So for now I'll just go to settings and let's check a couple of things here. So where was that system? So here it is in the system where you can adjust the memory you can just slide around but it has to be off. So the machine has to be for you to be able to adjust it. And then you need to go to storage. And this is where you need to hook up a Linux distribution in order to be able to install it onto a computer and onto a virtual machine. So I'll show you where to get that. Now again if you're going through these instructions you scroll down you'll be able to see more information on how to install it. And here's the download so you go to w w w boon to dot com Sly's downloads slash desktop just download it here. The theme of this is that it's actually very very big. You can support them if you like. You can donate here if you don't want to just say no. Take me to the download. I was going to start downloading but it takes a couple of hours. So be prepared for that. Yeah I know I was shocked too. Maybe it's just us truly an internet. Just click download here. It's not started. So here it is, it's one point four gigs. Well maybe it might be faster hopefully but for me to click a few hours the first time I know Australia Australian internet is not the best but we're getting there slowly we are getting that anyway. So once you die I canceled it because I already have that file. So once you've downloaded it go back here and where it is empty. Click this little icon. It's very like you might want to click this but you actually need to click this CD I can and then find that file that I so follow you downloaded. You just need to find it among your files on your computer. So if you click here you'll be able to actually go in and locate that file. I put it into my virtual box folder. But you can put it wherever you like. So there it is, you just double click and now it's connected. There you go. So it's all done. You can see you can remove it. If you don't want to have it there and that's it. You just click OK. And it's ready to go. What you'll find though is that the first time you launch it you might get an error and the error might look something like this. So I took a screenshot of it when I had it. Now I won't have it because I fixed it but you might get an error which looks like this which says basically that virtual machines are virtual environments have been disabled in at the level of the BIOS in your computer and that's you need to fix but you'll need to restart your whole computer in order to do that. So go ahead and try to launch it so let's see like you'll see in my case for instance that it's launching fine and this will start the installation process. As you get a second. So it's like any computer when you first install it. It's using That's virtual. Oh that is so file that we connected to install Linux right now starting installation and then you can walk through. So there we go. So you can see here you can actually go through the installation process. But before we do that, well basically once you get to the stage it's pretty straightforward from here you just go ahead and click install stillborns to and then you go through this process of installing it. Just go quickly and show you this part.

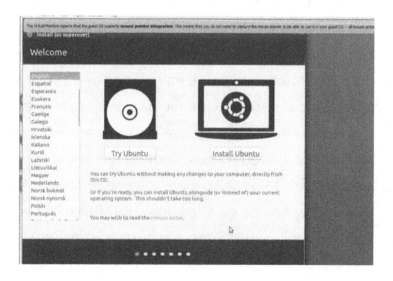

So continue on checking those boxes on your N-rays disk. Yes but don't worry this will only erase things inside this virtual machine not on your hard drive. So click Install now you click Continue. So I'm getting an error here because I just don't have enough space on my computer right now. So host them also look out for that as well. That just means you don't have enough space on your computer like we did allocate 50 gigabytes but on my actual hard drive right now I only have like nine gigabytes or something. So it's not an hour or even less than that. It's not enough to install So just be careful that you make sure you have enough. But once you want to ensure you have enough it will let you install the system onto the computer associates are going to power off. And the reason for that is because I already have another virtual box and am taking up some memory as well. In the meantime what I wanted to show you is how to sew it like. It's pretty straightforward from that part if you get to this situation you just go through insulation you know except the defaults and you'll have Linux on your virtual machine. But for now how do we deal with that error that we saw. So let me bring it up again so this area can restart your computer. I need to click depending on the machine. It's like one of the F-keys so two or three or four or five six eight 10 12 depending on the computer. But more very likely will be while your computers are starting you know when you look at the very start when you compute starting. You have the black screen because you need to get into the settings of the computer and look up your model of the motherboard or computer to find out what it is or what I do. I just press all of them. I just press one left to have three all of them at the same time. I don't recommend that because you might actually break something like that but that's the kind of approach I use sometimes when I like when I don't want to be researching what key I should be pressing. And so basically I'm just going to skip that part of the video that I recorded because I had to record on my phone because it's like obviously it's still before Windows loads. And I'll show you what it looks like and how to find that setting which we need to change. And then once you've changed that to just come back here and you can run your virtual machine, set up one. One last thing that mite's might change things is like if it's still working then some people play around with this checkbox that might do something for you but it wasn't necessary for me to check this checkbox. It's working fine after I've set it up and on the level of the BIOS. So there you go. I would just skip to that part of the video and see it. All right. So here I am in my B-L BIOS settings on my computer. So check this out. I'm going to go to the device. It's not, it's advanced. Then I'm going to click enter. If you set up and then if you look here you'll see virtualization technologies disabled. And so here we enter with a click enabled. No need to click save an exit that's f 10 for 8 10.

MAC OR LINUX INSTALLING ANACONDA

We're going to start by building a self-driving car so we'll create a map with a car and we will build an AI for the car. So we will basically put a brain in that car but that's not all we will have some other exciting challenges. We will also build some AI to beat some games like break out and doom and to do all this we're going to need not only Python but some integrated environments that contain all the packages that we need to build the AIS. So today in this Statoil we're going to start by installing Anaconda which is an idea that contains all the essential packages like non-prime that lead to implements and fighting codes. So that will help us a lot. But then unfortunately that won't be sufficient because you need to install some additional packages. But we will take care of that later. For now let's download and install Anaconda. So you just need to attack here and download the first link. There you go. And then you click on the first link download and it on that now. There you go. And you scroll down and then you will see this page where you can download an icon for the three systems: Windows, Mac OS or Linux. So I'm going to Maxson to stay there. And so now we have the choice between five and 3.6 and five and 2.7. And actually we're going to go for bison 2.7 and that's because as I told you we're going to install some extra packages like for example all the packages related to Cadie which will allow

162

us to make the Mac for the self-driving car. And since bison 3.6 is a recent version of Python. Well you have some of these packages that don't work yet. We're fighting 3.6. However they work very well with pipes and 2.7 and that's why we're going to go for five and 2.10. So let's go for it.

And then you can click on the graphical installer. Here we go. The download is running and then you have this offer for a cheat sheet. You can click on No thanks and now I just have to wait until the download is over and then we will be ready to install and I can go. So there we go. The download is over. So let's click on it. And this will bring us this window there we go. And so now basically that's very simple. You can just click on continue and continue again and can read the license agreement if you want. And if you agree you can click on agree and then install for me only and then you just need to take on Continue until you reach the summary and the end of the installation. I'm not doing it here because everything is already installed on my system. But you will definitely have no problem with it. OK so I'm going to close this once then I can do it. Well you can find it on your system and if you're on a Mac you will find it in your applications. But basically this is this one. And I can be the navigator. So you just click on it and then this will open Anaconda. OK. There we go. That's an icon that's welcome. And now you have the choice to open several programs so the two IDs I want to highlight here are a Jupyter notebook which is next an idea especially if you want to write a paper and you know include some mathematics in a later report. And that's besides executing your Python commands. But we won't be working with Jubouri, we will be working with Spider, which is another great idea in Anaconda. So as you can see this is a powerful bison ID with advanced editing, interactive testing, debugging and lots of other features. So let's go for it and therefore let's click on launch. This is a lunging spider. And there we go. Welcome to spider. It's about to open in seconds. And here we go. We are inside a spider. So the first thing that I want to highlight is that when you open a spire for the first time you will find this term that I found. This is just a temporary file and that is not the file where you should write and code.

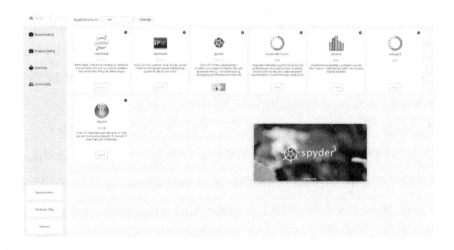

So the first thing you should do is go to the file at the top then open a new file and then close the 10:5. And that's a file that you can save in your working directory folder and run some Python code on it and then to save it that's the same file at the top. Then you click on Save us. All right then if you haven't done it already I recommend that you download the artificial intelligence it is that template folder of course. So you can find it in the LDS website that Curiel explains how to download in the previous project and once you have downloaded the folder you can go inside of it and you will find the three modules module one module to module three. And so now we're going to start with module one cell driving car and inside the full day you can save your life in fact that you have right now because we're going to set this folder as working directory and I highly recommend that you have your pipe and file inside the folder we set as a working directory. Things will be much easier after that. And then finally you can just give them to your files. Let's call it a DC for self-driving cars and then you can click on say perfect and then the important thing to say is that we are going to type all the code in this window. That's the editor window and that's from this window that will execute the code. Then once we execute the code the code will be executed here which is the account. So make sure you're using and I think console and not a classic bison can so and to do this you just need to go to view then panes and then make sure that I can so it's selected as well as your editor and variable Explorer that contains all the variables you will create when implementing the models. And then help if you want to get some help with one of the objects we create and file explore. And that leads me to the very important last point of spiders which is file explorers. So make sure that file explorer is selected. And then if that's the case let's go here file that for and that's basically the window that contains all your files on your computer. And why is that important? That's because this is from file explorer that will set the rightful heir as a working directory. So right now as you can see I'm on my desktop and that's artificial intelligence. It is a template folder of my desktop. So let's click on it then if you want to start implementing the self-driving car we go to module one self-driving car. And there you go. That's all the files that implemented the self-driving car. There is also the father to just save it as they see that why. That's this one. And now the last thing is to make sure this folder is set as a working directory. You can just click on the button here and then click on restart kernel. Then you click on. Yes and now you're all good. You have to write for a working directory and you are ready to start implementing our first AI. And this is going to be a self-driving car.

MAC OR LINUX INSTALLING PYTORCH AND KIVY

We are one step left from starting to build our AI for the soldier in the car. It is to be installed by torch and Katie so we're going to start with flight tours and first let me explain why we chose by torch rather than a sense of love for this course. Well that's because my torch is more powerful as opposed to a blow torch that can handle dynamic grass. That means that you have a graph of computations when you have to compute the gradients in the equations line behind artificial intelligence models. And this graph of conditions allows to compute very quickly the gradients and the composition functions. Indeed when you feed forward the signals in the neural network and when you back propagate the last error back into the neural network when you have these gradients that you have to compute these are the gradients of the last error with respect to the weights. And since we have several layers in the neural networks of the deeper nose Well you have to compute gradients of composition functions because you know one layer is expressed as a function of the previous layer which is expressed as a function of the previous previous layer. So you get these composition functions on which you have to compute the gradient. And that leads to nasty computations. But thanks to the dynamic graph that exists in by torche Well these considerations of the gradients of decomposition functions are done very efficiently. And so the consequence of all this is that by training with five torche Plus with a strong G-B your acceleration will be much faster and therefore you will be able to train your model much more efficiently. Thanks to these tiny graphs. So that's the main reason why we chose the torch. Besides it is really developed by the best teams in the world since indeed it is developed by Facebook and Invidia. So we're going to go with the torch and so let's install it right now. The good news is that the installation is very easy. First you have to go to this link towards that art and then you will find this page and then everything is very intuitive. First you choose the right system that you have. So it's either Linux or OSX. And if you're on Windows please follow the project made by Karylle on how to install a virtual machine to get a Linux system. And in that case you have to go here. As far as I'm concerned Amneris sex so I'm going to click here then. Package Manager I recommend to choose. So let's click on it then. So as you saw in the previous project we installed five and 2.70 we have to click here. And finally you can choose to install kuda as well. That's only if you have an Nvidia graphic card on your computer so you can check that in your system information. If you have any of you then you can click on the 8.0 and if that's not the case you can just click on. So I have a Mac which doesn't have an energy bill so I'm thinking about it. And then the rest is very simple. You just copy this first entry here.

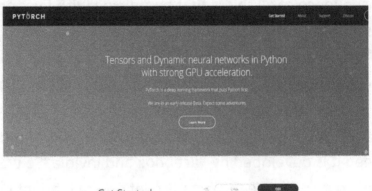

You just copy it and then you open a terminal there we go. You press enter and that's determined on you just have to paste the command line that you just copy and then press enter. I'm not going to press enter because my torch is already installed on my system but you just have to press enter. And this will install it automatically without any issue. All right and then you can also install torch vision but I don't think that's necessary I don't think you will be using it. But just in case you can install it as well. So that's the same you just face the command here and then press enter. All right. So I'm going to close the terminal and now by doing this you will have it installed on your system. And so now we can eventually say that you're ready to build an AI efficiently. Then the last thing we need to install and that's not related to building an AI AI but to make the app you know to make the self-driving car because we're going to make a map with a common app on which we will be able to draw some roads for the car to stay in. Well for this we need kiting. And so that's the second thing here. I'll provide the link right after this to an article. But that's the link you have to go to Cavitat or slash Ducs slash installation slash installation that you see now and then again you just have to find your system Windows OSX or Linux and then you just click on the right click. So I'm going to OSX and click on that. There we go. And then that's very easy. You just need to follow the instructions, just copy-paste the commands on your terminal and this will install KDE without any issue. So in this page you can see that you have several ways of installing KDE. You can install KDE using homebrew with. That's the first way you can install KDE using MacPorts with Pip. That's the second way so you have to choose between this one or that one. And you also have the third way which is using the caveat I don't really recommend that solution and in fact I recommend the first solution using homebrew with PIP so it doesn't matter whether you have homebrew already or not in your system. You can directly copy paste this command then based it on your terminal and press enter. Then you do the same for this command and then this command and then you don't have to run this command. This is just for the development version. So basically you just have to copy

171

paste one by one the three commands. This one this one and this one. And if you have any problem like something saying you don't have homebrew. Well I think you can click on it and this will lead you to homebrew and that's how you can and so humble. Again you just need to copy these commands based on a terminal and press enter.

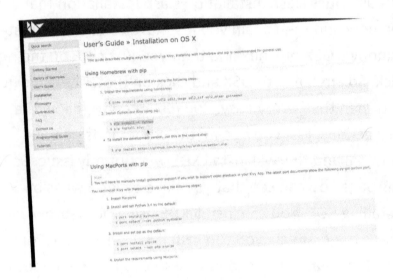

But I think it won't be necessary. I'm telling you this just in case. All right so now you're ready to go. You're ready not only to build an AI but also to make a self-driving car. It's going to be very exciting and quite challenging. We're going to do a lot of code. We're going to have three code files, two files to make the map you know with the Karnit and the movements of the car and some go to define the goals that the code will have to accomplish and some code that will make the connection between the map and the AI. And then we'll have the AI covered and that's the one we will implement step by step line by line so that you can clearly understand what's going on. And so that you can really become an expert in AI development. So I can't wait to start.

KIVY INSTALLATION WALK THROUGH MAC

How to get it set up on your machine for the purpose of this. We're using a higher version of pythoness because I've seen quite a few individuals using more than 3.5 3.6. And in addition I do think that thirty two point seven right now there has been a few Kivi related issues stemming from either an outdated X code site on versions usually the best option for that is to set a different version of installation of a previous version of Kiwi or sites. But for this we're going to walk through it we're going to set it up 3.5 us take a look at the first things first we have to install dependencies for Kivi so you can navigate to the Kiwi or informational page that tells you how to set it up or using homebrews or are we using the following command to our advantage. But first I want to actively live in a kind of environment. And I believe this is what it is called because I was working with a specific package. So let's see it returns, give it a second. Now I want to run the Bruegmann to install the required dependencies and let that run. And we will return once that set up once that set up we're going to be installing sites. And we're going to be installing Kivi as well. And attached to this lecture I will add a file as well that if anyone is using 2.70 is the recommended steps. If you do run into any errors or just if you're using whatever version of Python you run into any errors there's a few suggested solutions to work through it to get your TV set up as well.

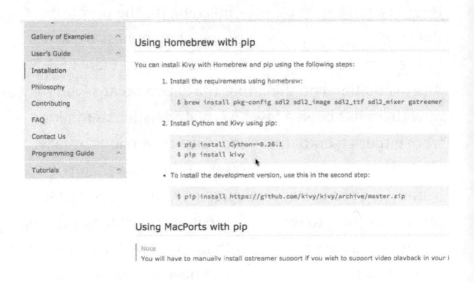

So as soon as homebrews set up we're going to be running this volume step and then install Kivi. It's pretty straightforward so we'll jump right back to it as soon as the dependencies are installed. I actually had them installed in this environment so we want to copy the following command. And we're going to install an icon. It should be a relatively quick install. But I will pause the video just in case. Now let's see it's collecting in. And while that runs we're going to go back. I mean you don't have to copy if you can remember to install a TV but sometimes it just makes it simple. And we're going to run the following command but let that run and return back to the video. All right. As you can see we have successfully installed TV. I did have some pre-installed packages in that environment so I guess I did luck out in that. All right. So we have that installed. I did look because I had some information already. Are some packages already compiled but you can scroll through the given information. Again if you run into any errors just double check the logs. The file that will attach and you can then run you know open spider or open a juror notebook and run a importante of it for me and you should be able to have it configured and ready to go. Right. Hope it helped you guys work through the installation again. Is pretty straightforward. Just these steps. If you do run into AGC see airfares make sure it's installed on your system or double check the version of the X code for Mac OS. Or you might need to update the command line tools from Apple. But overall I hope that helped you get installed. And as always if you have any questions please use non-discussion and we will get to them as soon as possible.

KIVY INSTALLATION WALK THROUGH LINUX

We're going to be installing Kivy on Linux. Two quick little walk through is actually pretty easy and simple and I'd say the most straightforward on Linux and one to operate the system. So to get started we need to pick either a bill we want a stable build and build. I'm going to use the stable build. So we're going to copy the following command and we're to open a terminal for mine. I do have one already but we're just going to go through a walk through the installation command. This is going to be an operating room. If you have your environment in common you can always use the source activate. And then name your environment command to get your environment working. But for now it's me running through there. So we're going to pace that we face that. All right. I'm running sudo so you have to enter the password. Since it is a pseudo command to press enter.

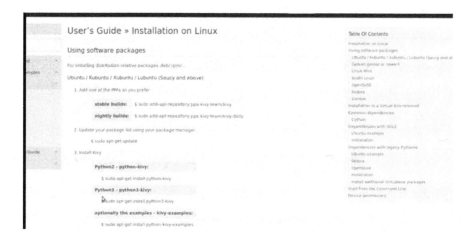

Using software packages

For installing distribution relative packages .deb/.rpm/...

Ubuntu / Kubuntu / Xubuntu / Lubuntu (Saucy and above)

1. Add one of the PPAs as you prefer

stable builds: $ sudo add-apt-repository ppa:kivy-team/kivy

nightly builds: $ sudo add-apt-repository ppa:kivy-team/kivy-daily

2. Update your package list using your package manager

$ sudo apt-get update

3. Install Kivy

Python2 - python-kivy:

$ sudo apt-get install python-kivy

Python3 - python3-kivy:

$ sudo apt-get install python3-kivy

optionally the examples - kivy-examples:

$ sudo apt-get install python-kivy-examples

All right. We're going to go back. We need to update our package manager. So again copy it back to your terminal. Paste it. Everything should be up to date with that wrong. Well that runs you need to use the following interviews in place to use this one using Python 3. You can use just one when using Python 3. So copy this and we're going to piece it in and that's it. So the head can be installed pretty well. It was much quicker. You know Kiv you might just take a little bit longer. Since it does have some packages it's going to run through to install a new machine. But again it's straightforward these you know mainly through steps. Just make sure you are using Python to use the Python to come in the future in Python 3. Use a Python 3 command. You are running sudo so you need the password to have that privilege. If you're operating in a specific area. Make sure you launch the excuse me environment beforehand. And now you can open fire or you can open a Juber notebook you know of any other kind of applications and you'll be able to run Kivi. All right. Hope that helped walk through the installation steps for you.

GETTING STARTED

Now that you have a torch and can be installed on your system. We are ready to start implementing the self-driving car and I can tell you we have an exciting adventure ahead of us. So the first thing we're going to do now before we start is set the right for those working directory. That's very important because we are going to have three files to implement this car and all the cars are connected to each other. So when you execute the file it will take classes , functions and objects from another file and this other file has to be in the same working directory as the file that you're executing. That's why it's very important to have one simple folder with all the files and that is your working directory folder. So let's just get this done. And then we will be able to start. So the first thing you do is go to 5: 4 here. That's this window. And then you will probably be on your desktop. So right now you can see them on my desktop or maybe even your documents. But anyway you have to find the folder that contains your artificial intelligence. It is that template folder that you downloaded from the Web site that will walk you through it. So just find this folder then open it from file explorer then go to module one self-driving car and then there you go. This Mudgal one cell shopping cart folder contains three files that's the three files that are connected to each other to implement not only the self-driving car on the map but also the brain of the car that is the AI that will be integrated to the car. And so this folder containing these three files is your working directory folder. And now to make sure that this folder is set in its working directory. You can click on the two buttons here and then restart the kernel. Then you can click on yes and there you go. Now you are 100 percent sure that this for the content in your three files is that as a working directory.

```python
1 # Self Driving Car
2
3 # Importing the libraries
4 import numpy as np
5 from random import random, randint
6 import matplotlib.pyplot as plt
7 import time
8
9 # Importing the Kivy packages
10 from kivy.app import App
11 from kivy.uix.widget import Widget
12 from kivy.uix.button import Button
13 from kivy.graphics import Color, Ellipse, Line
14 from kivy.config import Config
15 from kivy.properties import NumericProperty, ReferenceListProperty, ObjectProperty
16 from kivy.vector import Vector
17 from kivy.clock import Clock
18
19 # Importing the Dqn object from our AI in ai.py
20 from ai import Dqn
21
22 # Adding this line if we don't want the right click to put a red point
23 Config.set('input', 'mouse', 'mouse,multitouch_on_demand')
24
25 # Introducing last_x and last_y, used to keep the last point in memory when we draw
26 last_x = 0
27 last_y = 0
28 n_points = 0
29 length = 0
30
31 # Getting our AI, which we call "brain", and that contains our neural network that
32 brain = Dqn(5,3,0.9)
33 action2rotation = [0,20,-20]
34 last_reward = 0
35 scores = []
36
37 # Initializing the map
38 first_update = True
39 def init():
40     global sand
41     global goal_x
42     global goal_y
43     global first_update
44     sand = np.zeros((longueur,largeur))
45     goal_x = 20
46     goal_y = largeur - 20
47     first_update = False
48
49 # Initializing the last distance
50 last_distance = 0
51
```

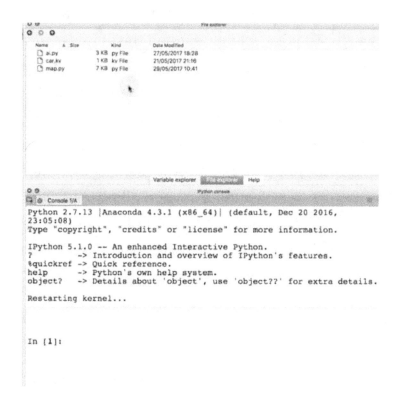

```
                                          File explorer
○  ○  ○
 Name      ▲ Size        Kind            Date Modified
 □ ai.py         3 KB  py File      27/05/2017 18:28
 □ car.kv        1 KB  kv File      21/05/2017 21:16
 □ map.py        7 KB  py File      29/05/2017 10:41




                        Variable explorer  File explorer   Help
○ ○                                 Python console
   ○  Console 1/A
Python 2.7.13 |Anaconda 4.3.1 (x86_64)| (default, Dec 20 2016,
23:05:08)
Type "copyright", "credits" or "license" for more information.

IPython 5.1.0 -- An enhanced Interactive Python.
?          -> Introduction and overview of IPython's features.
%quickref -> Quick reference.
help       -> Python's own help system.
object?    -> Details about 'object', use 'object??' for extra details.

Restarting kernel...


In [1]:
```

OK. And so now before we start I would just like to explain quickly what these three valves are. So as you probably recognized the first one here. Why is the file that contains the brain of the car? So you know that's in this file that will implement the artificial intelligence that will be integrated to the card. So that's why I'm calling it the brain of the car because this artificial intelligence is based on a neural network. So it will be like your car will have a neural network inside of it. That's why the electrical brain. Then the second file here occasionally finds a car that Katie and you cannot open in here. But you can open it from a text editor and actually that's what

I'm going to do right now. I'm opening it with subcontext. There we go. That is sublime text and this is this card that cavy fell open and subcontext. For those of you who are on Windows you can open it with notepad plus plus. So here is what the character looks like. We're not going to focus on it in this course because this is only related to KDE but basically to understand what's going on here. Well as you can see we create several objects that will be on the map. So for example this first object here is the car and for this car you can find some valuables like the angle that is the angle of rotation. Then you can define the shape that you want your car to have. So this will be a rectangle like the basic shape of a car. Then you have some other objects that will want to involve three. So these three balls here will be as you will see later the sensors of the car because the car will have sensors that will detect if there are some obstacles around the car. So these rebels here are just to highlight the sensors on the car. So we will see them and besides I set a different color for each of them. And then we have a last object which is to connect all the previous objects together to make the car because the sensors will be attached to the car so that when the car moves well the sensor moves as well. All right but this is not the most important here so we are going to move on to Boston. This is just to show you what cable looks like. And this Fall of course will be connected to our other files. And mostly it will be connected to the third file. Not that way, which is this one right here in

Nevada. Why is it? Well this is where we make the whole map and also the whole game because you will see that we'll be playing some games with the car. You know we will give it some challenges like avoiding some obstacles or doing some round trips between two destinations on a more and more difficult road. So we will make a game and that game happens in this big fall here. So this fall is important, therefore we're going to see it in detail. However since this is not directly related to AA I will not go to it line by line. I will just explain each line of code. Besides the template for that you'll find the same code as this one but commented. So each line of code will be tormented. So that's if you're interested in knowing how to develop a game within the application. Well you will be able to understand anything that we do here. But what's important also is that not only do we make the map in the game but also we make some important connections between the map and the future that he will implement afterwards. And by the way this is much more important and therefore we will implement it step by step. We will write together each of these lines of code. But for math I will just describe all the code sections here and that's what I will do in the next section right after this project. I think the next two projects are important for you to understand the connection between the map and the AI.

SELF DRIVING CAR - STEP 1

So in just a toilet I'm going to explain the environment on which we will implement our artificial intelligence and that will contain Of course the car that will train to drive itself and to avoid obstacles and on which will draw some roads and some blocks for our cars to navigate around them. So we will later build this artificial intelligence to train this car to drive on the road you know without crossing the limits and avoiding some obstacles that will be put inside the road. So this is a pretty exciting challenge. And actually there are two separate files as you can see there is the apex and fowl that are artificial intelligence that will do all the training to train the car how to sell drive. And we have a map that we found that is the code that makes all this environment. So here is that code that's actually 200 lines of code a little more. So this code is not typically related to AI. It is just a code to make the environment make the map. So I'm going to go through each of the sections one by one to explain but we're not going to implement this code line by line from scratch because we want to focus on artificial intelligence. But let's still go through the sections one by one to understand what's happening. So first we import the central libraries that's for any code. We need some libraries to perform some tasks more efficiently than importing all the cavy packages. So that's not very important because this is all specific to Cavey we're using cavy to make the map. And so we're importing a lot of classes and objects to be able to make this map and add some tools in the map. All right then this line is important. This line is related because basically this is where we import our brain, the brain of the car which will be another jet of this did you in class and the teacher in class. Is our artificial intelligence itself? You will see we will implement the dequeue in class in the following projects. And as you might have guessed, dequeue instances for deep Q networks. So we will implement a deque learning network and then once it's ready we will be importing it here with this line from the AI and the eyes of course are a python file. All right. So I can't wait to implement this. This is going to be quite a journey but you will see this is going to be very exciting because thanks to the I the car will be able to drive itself. All right. And now before I move on to the next sections we have to explain how we will train this car. I'm not going to explain the neural network right now but I'm going to explain the idea of how we can train the car to drive itself and to avoid obstacles. So you know in real life if you want to train a real car to avoid some walls or some obstacles. Well what would you do? You would definitely not take real walls or real big obstacles and smash your car onto them. That would cost you a lot of money. Instead a more intelligent idea would be to punish your car not when it smashes a wall or an obstacle but when it goes onto some sand. So it's like you have a field. This field has some roads on which the car has to stay and the roads are delimited by some sand. And each time the car goes into the center it's like it's going on to an obstacle because once the car goes into some sand it will be slowed down and we will make sure that the car that is penalized is punished for that. And that is one essential point of artificial intelligence. The bad word comes whenever the car goes into some sense and is slowed down. All right. And therefore here I'm introducing the last text and that's why. Which are the coordinates of the last point in memory when we draw some scent on the map. All right. And then we get our artificial intelligence which we call brain and that contains our neural network and we will call it brain because this is actually the brain of the car and that contains our Noodle Network. All right. So in this line of code as you can see I'm creating objects for the teacher in class. I will remind you that classes and objects are but Brenna's the object dehumanizes the class and 5:3 and 0.9 are the inputs of the class. So that's very simple: five corresponds to the states that are encoded vectors of five dimensions. We will see what they are perfectly describing what's happening in the environment on the map. Then there is the number of actions there will be three possible actions: go left , go straight or go right and 0.9 is again a parameter in the dequeue learning algorithm. All right and then we have the action through rotation. So action to rotation is a vector of three elements. 020 and minus 20. And so we have to do this because the actions are encoded by three numbers 0 1 and 2 and that corresponds to the indexes of this action two rotation vector. So for example if the action that is selected at time t is zero. Well zero corresponds to the index of this action two rotation vector and the value of index 0 is zero. And therefore we will go straight then if the action selected is 1. Well one corresponds to the index of this action two additional vectors and the value of this vector that has a next one is 20. So 20 corresponds to a rotation of 20 degrees and that means the code will go 20 degrees to the right and then if the action selected is too good to correspond to the index of this action to the rotation vector. And therefore the code will do a rotation of minus 20 degrees and therefore it will go to the left. All right then we introduce the left reward Voivode because at each stage will be getting the last word. So remember if the card doesn't go into some sense then the reward will be positive. And if the code goes on to some sense well it will get the bad reward and each time this variable will contain this reward that it gets H20.

```python
1 # Self Driving Car
2
3 # Importing the libraries
4 import numpy as np
5 from random import random, randint
6 import matplotlib.pyplot as plt
7 import time
8
9 # Importing the Kivy packages
10 from kivy.app import App
11 from kivy.uix.widget import Widget
12 from kivy.uix.button import Button
13 from kivy.graphics import Color, Ellipse, Line
14 from kivy.config import Config
15 from kivy.properties import NumericProperty, ReferenceListProperty, ObjectProperty
16 from kivy.vector import Vector
17 from kivy.clock import Clock
18
19 # Importing the Dqn object from our AI in ai.py
20 from ai import Dqn
21
22 # Adding this line if we don't want the right click to put a red point
23 Config.set('input', 'mouse', 'mouse,multitouch_on_demand')
24
25 # Introducing last_x and last_y, used to keep the last point in memory when we draw t
26 last_x = 0
27 last_y = 0
28 n_points = 0
29 length = 0
30
31 # Getting our AI, which we call "brain", and that contains our neural network that re
32 brain = Dqn(5,3,0.9)
33 action2rotation = [0,20,-20]
34 last_reward = 0
35 scores = []
36
37 # Initializing the map
38 first_update = True
39 def init():
40     global sand
41     global goal_x
42     global goal_y
43     global first_update
44     sand = np.zeros((longueur,largeur))
45     goal_x = 20
46     goal_y = largeur-20
47     first_update = False
48
49 # Initializing the last distance
50 last_distance = 0
```

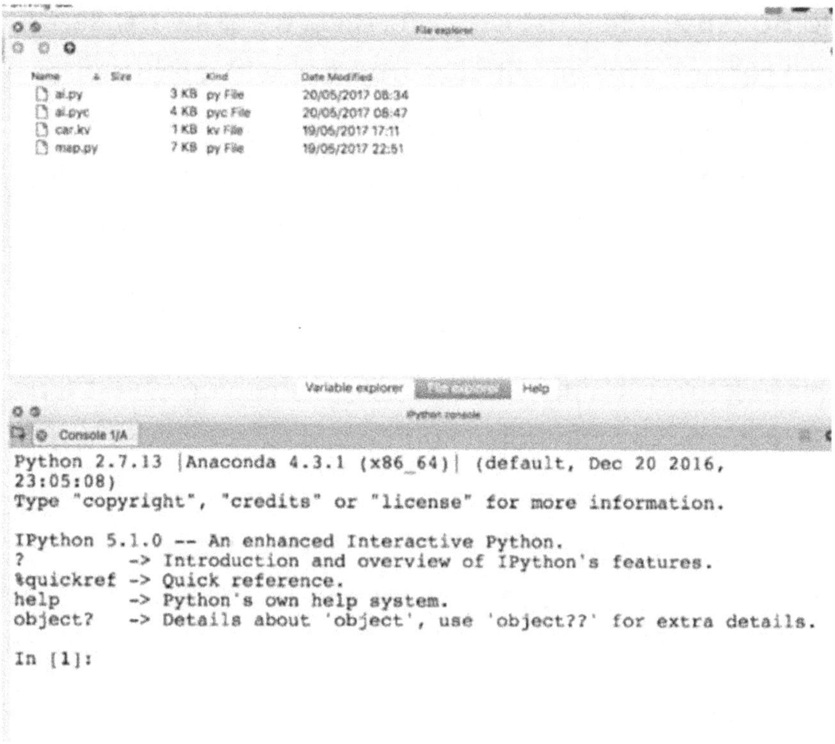
Name
Size
Kind
Date Modified
ai.py
3 KB
py File
20/05/2017 08:34
ai.pyc
4 KB
pyc File
20/05/2017 08:47
car.kv
1 KB
kv File
19/05/2017 17:11
map.py
7 KB
py File
19/05/2017 22:51
Variable explorer
Help
Console 1/A
Python 2.7.13 |Anaconda 4.3.1 (x86_64)| (default, Dec 20 2016, 23:05:08)
Type "copyright", "credits" or "license" for more information.
IPython 5.1.0 -- An enhanced Interactive Python.
? -> Introduction and overview of IPython's features.
%quickref -> Quick reference.
help -> Python's own help system.
object? -> Details about 'object', use 'object??' for extra details.
In [1]:

And then we initialize the scores which is a vector that will contain the reward. Not all of them but the reward. Onto a sliding window so that you know we can make a curve of the mean squat the reward with respect to time. All right then in this code section we initialize the map so we initialize. For example the said variable. So that's important. The second variable is actually going to be an array in which the cells will be the pixels of the map and in each cell we will have a 1. If there is some sense in a zero if there is no center at the beginning we will not be drawing anything. So there will be no sense at all and therefore all the cells of the center array will have a zero.

There will be zeros everywhere and as soon as we draw some sense while the cells on which we draw the sense will get one and we initialize the race with all the zeros right here sent equals and zeros. Then we have this important thing which is the goal. So the goal is a point in the map which will train the car to reach. So it's like a destination. So what is this goal going to be? Well this is going to be the upper left corner of the map to train the car to go to the upper left corner of the map. And then once it reaches the upper left corner of the map then we will tend to go to the bottom right corner of the map so we can imagine the following scenario. The upper left corner of the map is the airport of a city and the bottom right corner of the map is the downtown of the city. And we will train a taxi or Uber to do some round trips between the airport and downtown. And of course we'll make the task difficult for this taxi by drawing some more and more difficult roads and adding more and more obstacles on the street to see if the taxi can still manage to go from the airport to downtown. So this is going to be fun. And so that's why here I'm setting the coordinates of the first goal that is the airport which is at the upper left of the screen. So the map will be like a square like this and the coordinates of the origin that is the coordinates 00 is right here. And then larger is this distance here. So the coordinates 20 and Najah minus 20 will therefore be right here in the upper left corner of the map.

```python
 4 import numpy as np
 5 from random import random, randint
 6 import matplotlib.pyplot as plt
 7 import time
 8
 9 # Importing the Kivy packages
10 from kivy.app import App
11 from kivy.uix.widget import Widget
12 from kivy.uix.button import Button
13 from kivy.graphics import Color, Ellipse, Line
14 from kivy.config import Config
15 from kivy.properties import NumericProperty, ReferenceListProperty, ObjectProperty
16 from kivy.vector import Vector
17 from kivy.clock import Clock
18
19 # Importing the Dqn object from our AI in ai.py
20 from ai import Dqn
21
22 # Adding this line if we don't want the right click to put a red point
23 Config.set('input', 'mouse', 'mouse,multitouch_on_demand')
24
25 # Introducing last_x and last_y, used to keep the last point in memory when we draw the sand
26 last_x = 0
27 last_y = 0
28 n_points = 0
29 length = 0
30
31 # Getting our AI, which we call "brain", and that contains our neural network that represents
32 brain = Dqn(5,3,0.9)
33 action2rotation = [0,20,-20]
34 last_reward = 0
35 scores = []
36
37 # Initializing the map
38 first_update = True
39 def init():
40     global sand
41     global goal_x
42     global goal_y
43     global first_update
44     sand = np.zeros((longueur,largeur))
45     goal_x = 20
46     goal_y = largeur-20
47     first_update = False
48
49 # Initializing the last distance
50 last_distance = 0
51
52 # Creating the car class
53
54 class Car(Widget):
```

191

And why did I choose 20 and not zero. Well that's because we want to train the car not to rush into the walls. You know we want to train into the walls as well and therefore it's not zero because we don't want the car to touch where we want to go. So we have to put it right here and then I'm just introducing the last distance variable which just gives the current distance from the car to the road and that I'm initializing to zero. All right. And now time to make the car and the game. So we're going to make two classes, one class for the car and one class for the game. And inside these classes will already make some connections with our AI.

SELF DRIVING CAR - STEP 2

And now time for the exciting stuff we create the car and we do that with a class of course. You will see that the class is very practical to create some things that have a lot of properties because as you can see not only finding some variables from my car but also some functions which of course is the function that will make the car move from left to right or going straight. So we have a couple of variables that are important to describe the environment we have for example the angle which is the angle between the x axis and the axis of the direction of the car. Then we have the rotation which is its last rotation which remember is either 0 degree 20 degrees or minus 20 degrees. Then we have the velocity, the x coordinate of the velocity vector and the y coordinate of the velocity vector. And then the vector of coordinates velocity x and velocity Y then we have the sensors and the signals. And that's very important. The call that we're making will have three sensors: one sensor two and sensor three sensors one will be detecting if there is any sense in front of the car. Then sensor 2 is the sensor that will detect if there is any sense at the left of the car and sensor 3 is the sensor that will detect if there is any sense at the right of the car. And then from these three sensors we get the signals that are received by each of the sensors.

```python
27 last_y = 0
28 n_points = 0
29 length = 0
30
31 # Getting our AI, which we call "brain", and that contains our neural
32 brain = Dqn(5,3,0.9)
33 action2rotation = [0,20,-20]
34 last_reward = 0
35 scores = []
36
37 # Initializing the map
38 first_update = True
39 def init():
40     global sand
41     global goal_x
42     global goal_y
43     global first_update
44     sand = np.zeros((longueur,largeur))
45     goal_x = 20
46     goal_y = largeur-20
47     first_update = False
48
49 # Initializing the last distance
50 last_distance = 0
51
52 # Creating the car class
53
54 class Car(Widget):
55
56     angle = NumericProperty(0)
57     rotation = NumericProperty(0)
58     velocity_x = NumericProperty(0)
59     velocity_y = NumericProperty(0)
60     velocity = ReferenceListProperty(velocity_x, velocity_y)
61     sensor1_x = NumericProperty(0)
62     sensor1_y = NumericProperty(0)
63     sensor1 = ReferenceListProperty(sensor1_x, sensor1_y)
64     sensor2_x = NumericProperty(0)
65     sensor2_y = NumericProperty(0)
66     sensor2 = ReferenceListProperty(sensor2_x, sensor2_y)
67     sensor3_x = NumericProperty(0)
68     sensor3_y = NumericProperty(0)
69     sensor3 = ReferenceListProperty(sensor3_x, sensor3_y)
70     signal1 = NumericProperty(0)
71     signal2 = NumericProperty(0)
72     signal3 = NumericProperty(0)
73
74     def move(self, rotation):
75         self.pos = Vector(*self.velocity) + self.pos
76         self.rotation = rotation
77         self.angle = self.angle + self.rotation
```

194

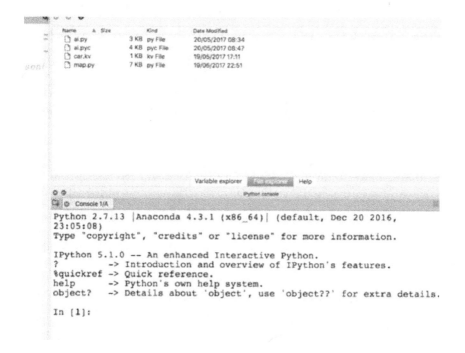

```
Name          Size     Kind         Date Modified
ai.py         3 KB     py File      20/05/2017 08:34
ai.pyc        4 KB     pyc File     20/05/2017 08:47
car.kv        1 KB     kv File      19/05/2017 17:11
map.py        7 KB     py File      19/06/2017 22:51
```

Variable explorer   File explorer   Help

Python console

Console 1/A

```
Python 2.7.13 |Anaconda 4.3.1 (x86_64)| (default, Dec 20 2016,
23:05:08)
Type "copyright", "credits" or "license" for more information.

IPython 5.1.0 -- An enhanced Interactive Python.
?               -> Introduction and overview of IPython's features.
%quickref -> Quick reference.
help          -> Python's own help system.
object?    -> Details about 'object', use 'object??' for extra details.

In [1]:
```

So signal one is the signal received by sensor one signal to is the signal received by sensor 2 and signal 3 is the signal received by sensor 3. And so how does it work? Signal 1 is the density of send around sensor one signal to is the density of center around sensor to signal three is the density of sent around sensitivity and how do we compute this density of sand. Well that's very simple. We take some big squares around each of the sensors. These are actually squares of 200 by 200 and for each of the squares we divide the number of ones in the square by the total number of cells in the square that is 22 and 20 equals 400. And that gives us the density of sand because the ones correspond to the center. We do this for each sensor and that gives us the density of sand around each sensor. That is the signal. All right so now we have everything to detect the sensor and then we have the move function. And of course the move function is what will allow the core to go to the left going straight or going to the right. So let's go through it quickly. We have here the update of the position of the car with its last position which is self the pass here and the velocity vector. So thanks to the velocity vector the position will be updated in the direction of the velocity vector. Then we get the rotation which we will get further down in the code right here. Rotation equals action to rotation action. He will select the action and then get in the rotation. And so this self-protection equals rotation here. It's this rotation that we get to know how we need to rotate the car that is going to the left or to the right. Then we update the angle which I remember is the angle between the x axis and the axis of the direction of the car. And then once the car has moved then we have to update the sensors and the signal because of course when the car has just rotated while the sensors have rotated as well and therefore we need to rotate them by using the rotate function and to which we add the new position. And why do we have this vector of 30 0. Well that's simply because 30 is the distance between the car and the sensor. You know the distance between the car and what the car detects. And then once the sensors are updated Well then it's time to update the signals. And so here we do exactly what I explained to you computer signals. We give the x coordinates of our sensor then we take all the cells from Manston to plus 10 then we do the same for the y coordinate taking all the cells from Madison to plus 10. So therefore we get the square of 20 by 20 pixels surrounding the sensor and inside the square we have some older ones. So basically with some of the cells because the cells contain 0 or 1 and since in a 20 by 20 square there is 20 times 20 equals 400 cells. Well we divide it by 400 to get the density of ones inside the square and that's how we get the signal of the density of centers around the sensor and we do the same for the second sensor and the third sensor to get the second signal and the third signal. OK. So that's to take the sensor and then these three lines of code here are very important. It's another that we want to get to our car when it's reaching one of the edges of the map.

```
50 last_distance = 0
51
52 # Creating the car class
53
54 class Car(Widget):
55
56     angle = NumericProperty(0)
57     rotation = NumericProperty(0)
58     velocity_x = NumericProperty(0)
59     velocity_y = NumericProperty(0)
60     velocity = ReferenceListProperty(velocity_x, velocity_y)
61     sensor1_x = NumericProperty(0)
62     sensor1_y = NumericProperty(0)
63     sensor1 = ReferenceListProperty(sensor1_x, sensor1_y)
64     sensor2_x = NumericProperty(0)
65     sensor2_y = NumericProperty(0)
66     sensor2 = ReferenceListProperty(sensor2_x, sensor2_y)
67     sensor3_x = NumericProperty(0)
68     sensor3_y = NumericProperty(0)
69     sensor3 = ReferenceListProperty(sensor3_x, sensor3_y)
70     signal1 = NumericProperty(0)
71     signal2 = NumericProperty(0)
72     signal3 = NumericProperty(0)
73
74     def move(self, rotation):
75         self.pos = Vector(*self.velocity) + self.pos
76         self.rotation = rotation
77         self.angle = self.angle + self.rotation
78         self.sensor1 = Vector(30, 0).rotate(self.angle) + self.pos
79         self.sensor2 = Vector(30, 0).rotate((self.angle+30)%360) + self.pos
80         self.sensor3 = Vector(30, 0).rotate((self.angle-30)%360) + self.pos
81         self.signal1 = int(np.sum(sand[int(self.sensor1_x)-10:int(self.sensor1_x)+10, int(s
82         self.signal2 = int(np.sum(sand[int(self.sensor2_x)-10:int(self.sensor2_x)+10, int(s
83         self.signal3 = int(np.sum(sand[int(self.sensor3_x)-10:int(self.sensor3_x)+10, int(s
84         if self.sensor1_x>longueur-10 or self.sensor1_x<10 or self.sensor1_y>largeur-10 or
85             self.signal1 = 1.
86         if self.sensor2_x>longueur-10 or self.sensor2_x<10 or self.sensor2_y>largeur-10 or
87             self.signal2 = 1.
88         if self.sensor3_x>longueur-10 or self.sensor3_x<10 or self.sensor3_y>largeur-10 or
89             self.signal3 = 1.
90
91 class Ball1(Widget):
92     pass
93 class Ball2(Widget):
94     pass
95 class Ball3(Widget):
96     pass
97
98 # Creating the game class
99
100 class Game(Widget):
```

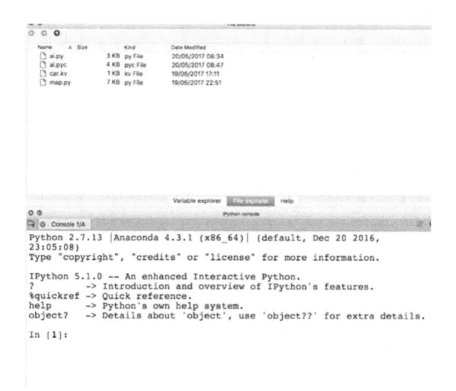

```
Name          ▲ Size        Kind          Date Modified
  ai.py          3 KB  py File      20/05/2017 08:34
  ai.pyc         4 KB  pyc File     20/05/2017 08:47
  car.kv         1 KB  kv File      19/06/2017 17:11
  map.py         7 KB  py File      19/06/2017 22:51
```

```
                     Variable explorer   File explorer   Help
                              Python console
  Console 1/A

Python 2.7.13 |Anaconda 4.3.1 (x86_64)| (default, Dec 20 2016,
23:05:08)
Type "copyright", "credits" or "license" for more information.

IPython 5.1.0 -- An enhanced Interactive Python.
?          -> Introduction and overview of IPython's features.
%quickref -> Quick reference.
help       -> Python's own help system.
object?    -> Details about 'object', use 'object??' for extra details.

In [1]:
```

You know we don't want the car to rush into some walls and therefore we want to penalize it to punish it when it's getting too close to the Wall and therefore that's what we do here. If the first sensor is larger than longer minus 10 that is larger than here because longer is this distance here so longer minus 10 is right here. So if sensor one acts larger than longer Mansion concerns all the points are here. That is if the car is getting closer to the right edge of the map or if cell sensor one acts lower than 10 that's right here if the car is getting closer to the left edge of the map or if sensor Y is larger than larger minus 10 that's the upper edge of the map and or if self-censored Y is lower than 10 that is the lower edge of the map. And so if the sensor one is reaching any of these four edges Well we will put the signal of the sensor signal when the signal sent one. We will set it to be one. And what does that mean? That means full sound like the full density of sand. It's like the worst you could get. There's so much sense that it's going to stop your car. So the signal will be one and therefore the car will get a terribly bad reward. All right. And then we do the same for signals too and signal three from sensor two instances three. All right. And then we create the game class so that's basically the class to create the game because so far we have only created the car and now of course we have to create the map. We have to create the game itself. So we will not be playing the game, it's our AI that will be playing the game and the game is actually to avoid obstacles and to go from the airport to downtown and vice versa. So in this game class we need to create some objects like the car then we need to define the update function. That is the most important and actually we will focus on that right now because that's in this update function that will select the action that the car has to do and each time to accomplish its goal. And this action is exactly the output of our neural network. The new will that work that will be at the heart of our artificial intelligence. And so this action is returned by the brain of the car which remains the object of our human class that will be made in our AI file. And this object has a method that is called update and it takes as input the last word and the last signal. So the last word is of course the last word attained by the car and the last signal is of course the last signal of the three sensors signal one from sensor one signal two from sensor to signal three from sensor 3. But then I'm adding two other inputs which are the orientation of the car with respect to the goal.

```
107 serve_car(self):
108 self.car.center = self.center
109 self.car.velocity = Vector(6, 0)
110
111 update(self, dt):
112
113 global brain
114 global last_reward
115 global scores
116 global last_distance
117 global goal_x
118 global goal_y
119 global longueur
120 global largeur
121
122 longueur = self.width
123 largeur = self.height
124 if first_update:
125     init()
126
127 xx = goal_x - self.car.x
128 yy = goal_y - self.car.y
129 orientation = Vector(*self.car.velocity).angle((xx,yy))/180.
130 last_signal = [self.car.signal1, self.car.signal2, self.car.signal3, orientation, -orientati
131 action = brain.update(last_reward, last_signal)
132 scores.append(brain.score())
133 rotation = action2rotation[action]
134 self.car.move(rotation)
135 distance = np.sqrt((self.car.x - goal_x)**2 + (self.car.y - goal_y)**2)
136 self.ball1.pos = self.car.sensor1
137 self.ball2.pos = self.car.sensor2
138 self.ball3.pos = self.car.sensor3
139
140 if sand[int(self.car.x),int(self.car.y)] > 0:
141     self.car.velocity = Vector(1, 0).rotate(self.car.angle)
142     last_reward = -1
143 else:   # otherwise
144     self.car.velocity = Vector(6, 0).rotate(self.car.angle)
145     last_reward = -0.2
146     if distance < last_distance:
147         last_reward = 0.1
148
149 if self.car.x < 10:
150     self.car.x = 10
151     last_reward = -1
152 if self.car.x > self.width-10:
153     self.car.x = self.width-10
154     last_reward = -1
155 if self.car.y < 10:
156     self.car.y = 10
157     last reward = -1
```

So for example if the car is heading towards the goal then the orientation will be equal to zero. If it goes slightly to the right then the orientation will be close to 45 degrees. And if it goes slightly to the left the orientation will be close to minus 45 degrees. So that's the force input of our input states. And then there is a lesson which is minus orientation. So usually the inputs of a neural network are independent. There is no multicollinearity but it doesn't really matter if we are this because the neural network will just fix that with the weights. But still I notice that by adding this minus orientation well that allows the car the training of the car to stabilize the acceleration. You know what we're doing is that the AI doesn't always explore in the same direction by adding this minus orientation. We make sure that it explores in both directions, right or left. And so these three signals Plus the orientation and minus orientation are the five inputs of our encoded vector which will go into the network and our input vector that will go into the network and after it goes into the network Well the network returns the outputs which is the action to play. And each time and the output is returned by this update function that contains the network itself and the output of the network and therefore that's why we have to input the last signal that is the input state and also the last word because the action to play also depends on the last word. All right and then we update the main score of the words we update the rotation we use the move function to rotate the car according to the action that was selected. We take the distance of the car to the road and we will get the positions of the sensor ball one ball two in both Rieker responses to the balls that will represent the sensors on the map. You'll see that very quickly. And then here that part is very important because that's where we penalize the car if it goes into some sense because as you can see this means if the car is onto some sense well it will be slowed down. So that's where we reduce its velocity. You know its velocity is usually 6 as you can see here. And if it goes on to some sense it will be one which will be slowed down to 1. You'll see how the car will be slowed down once it goes into some sense. So it has slowed down. And besides it gets a bad reward it gets a minus one we want. And that's actually the worst reward you could get. The best reward is one, the worst word is minus one and the reward is between minus 1 and plus 1. And then otherwise. And the car isn't onto some sand. Well it keeps its usual speed of sex and then we add something else. If it's getting closer to the goal then it will get a slightly positive reward. And if it's getting further away from the goal Well it gets a slightly negative reward minus 0.2. And then last. Conditions that are related to the reward. Well that's if the car is getting too close to one of the edges as we spoke of earlier. Remember when we talked about fuel sensors. Well if the car is getting too close to the left edge of the map it gets minus one word if it gets too close to the right edge of the map it gets rewarded minus one. And if it gets too close to the bottom edge of the map it gets you or minus one. And if it gets too close to the upper left of the map it gets rewards minus one. So that's a terrible punishment. And so you will see how it's full and fast not to rush into something else. All right and then this is to update the go when the goal is reached. So you know when the car reaches the airport which is the first go there is the upper left corner of the map. While the goal changes to the bottom right corner of the map which is downtown. And that's exactly what we do here: we update the x coordinate of the Crow and the white coordinates of the call and then we update the distance from the car to the car.

```
120        global largeur
121
122        longueur = self.width
123        largeur = self.height
124        if first_update:
125            init()
126
127        xx = goal_x - self.car.x
128        yy = goal_y - self.car.y
129        orientation = Vector(*self.car.velocity).angle((xx,yy))/180.
130        last_signal = [self.car.signal1, self.car.signal2, self.car.signal3, orientation, -c
131        action = brain.update(last_reward, last_signal)
132        scores.append(brain.score())
133        rotation = action2rotation[action]
134        self.car.move(rotation)
135        distance = np.sqrt((self.car.x - goal_x)**2 + (self.car.y - goal_y)**2)
136        self.ball1.pos = self.car.sensor1
137        self.ball2.pos = self.car.sensor2
138        self.ball3.pos = self.car.sensor3
139
140        if sand[int(self.car.x),int(self.car.y)] > 0:
141            self.car.velocity = Vector(1, 0).rotate(self.car.angle)
142            last_reward = -1
143        else: # otherwise
144            self.car.velocity = Vector(6, 0).rotate(self.car.angle)
145            last_reward = -0.2
146            if distance < last_distance:
147                last_reward = 0.1
148
149        if self.car.x < 10:
150            self.car.x = 10
151            last_reward = -1
152        if self.car.x > self.width-10:
153            self.car.x = self.width-10
154            last_reward = -1
155        if self.car.y < 10:
156            self.car.y = 10
157            last_reward = -1
158        if self.car.y > self.height-10:
159            self.car.y = self.height-10
160            last_reward = -1
161
162        if distance < 100:
163            goal_x = self.width-goal_x
164            goal_y = self.height-goal_y
165        last_distance = distance
166
167 # Adding the painting tools
168
169 class MyPaintWidget(Widget):
```

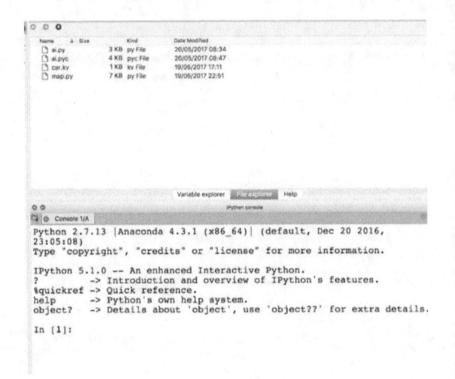

```
Name            ▲ Size        Kind        Date Modified
  ai.py           3 KB   py File    20/05/2017 08:34
  ai.pyc          4 KB   pyc File   20/05/2017 08:47
  car.kv          1 KB   kv File    19/05/2017 17:11
  map.py          7 KB   py File    19/05/2017 22:51
```

```
                          Variable explorer   File explorer   Help

                                      IPython console
  Console 1/A
Python 2.7.13 |Anaconda 4.3.1 (x86_64)| (default, Dec 20 2016,
23:05:08)
Type "copyright", "credits" or "license" for more information.

IPython 5.1.0 -- An enhanced Interactive Python.
?          -> Introduction and overview of IPython's features.
%quickref -> Quick reference.
help       -> Python's own help system.
object?    -> Details about 'object', use 'object??' for extra details.

In [1]:
```

All right. And then that's less important. That's just a class that will add the painting tools you know for us to be able to paint some roads or some obstacles on the map that's more related to K.V. you can have a look if you want. I'll provide the condensed version of this code and I'll provide some reference if you want to go deeper on how to do that with skivvy. But we're getting further from artificial intelligence so I'm not going to go into the details of it. And that's the same for the last code section with the car class that is just as the API buttons clear save and load. So that's what we do here. Clear canvas safe. And that's actually very important that's for us to be able to save the day I know to save the brain so that you can reuse it later by taking the load function which is another tool we add on the map to load the brain of the car that is to load the memory of the car how to navigate in the map. And then finally we have the last of the last code section which runs the whole thing that is which runs the map and the AI itself. And actually that's what we're going to do right now. Let's have a look at everything we made in this code. So right now the AI is not implemented. So the code will have a very random movement. It will actually look like an insect but don't worry we will fix that. Normally we will train it to move like a real car and train it to navigate following some roads and avoiding some obstacles. Let's do this. I'm going to select everything and execute. And here is the map. And here is the car. All right. So that's the little thing here that you see that looks like an insect in our car. So as I told you the actions are totally random. So each time the car selects randomly an action whether to go straight to the left or to the right. So that's why it is making some nonsense movements and that's why it's looking like an insect. So we will fix that of course. And of course since the AI is activated Well it is not going to the goal which is the airport here or to downtown at the bottom right of the map. And we will fix all this by making the AIs who will implement the AI into this car or this insect so you can see the three balls here: the yellow one, the red one and the white one. That's our three sensors. So that's what we'll detect. There is some scent around it. And speaking of scent Well let's throw some out. So to do so I just need to do a click left here and you know in some sense by still teaching left. So right now I'm adding some sand. We can add some more. So each time is insane as you can see by putting ones in the center array that's to send an array that's to 00 coordinates of the origin. And here there are a lot of them. And as you can see well that's good to see the car. We just went on to descend and slowed down. So as you can see right now it is really slow down because it's going into the sand. And right now it's trying to escape.

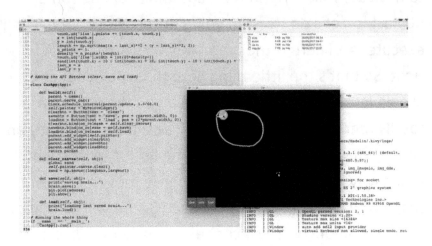

And so you know what we'll do is we will draw some roads and we will draw some roads from the airport to downtown and we will train the car to stay on the road and to avoid the obstacles. All right. And as you can see there is the clear button to clear the sand there is the save button to save the brain of the car. And actually there is this core curve that we spoke of, that safety that saves your model, actually the brain of your car and then you can know when you leave your cold or turn off your computer and you want to go back to it again. You can use the load button to load your mode, that is to load the brain and that will get the train AI of your car. All right so now I can't wait to start making the AI. This will be a lot of fun. We'll make our neural network and we will punish the car as soon as it doesn't do what we want. So let's do that from the next project.

SELF DRIVING CAR - STEP 3

All right so now we are going to implement artificial intelligence from scratch. We're going to cut it line by line. And in this first good section we're going to import the libraries. But before we start with this first code section I would like to explain the connection between the AI and our map. That is why we're implementing this for them. What is the purpose of our AI and where will we be using it? So it's actually very simple. We're only making our AI to select the right action each time. So OK we import the class from our file so we will be making this D2 in class in this file. But then we import it only to select the right action to play at each time and we select this action exactly at this line.

```
     a.py     0  map.py
 95 class Ball3(Widget):
 96     pass
 97
 98 # Creating the game class
 99
100 class Game(Widget):
101
102     car = ObjectProperty(None)
103     ball1 = ObjectProperty(None)
104     ball2 = ObjectProperty(None)
105     ball3 = ObjectProperty(None)
106
107     def serve_car(self):
108         self.car.center = self.center
109         self.car.velocity = Vector(6, 0)
110
111     def update(self, dt):
112
113         global brain
114         global last_reward
115         global scores
116         global last_distance
117         global goal_x
118         global goal_y
119         global longueur
120         global largeur
121
122         longueur = self.width
123         largeur = self.height
124         if first_update:
125             init()
126
127         xx = goal_x - self.car.x
128         yy = goal_y - self.car.y
129         orientation = Vector(*self.car.velocity).angle((xx,yy))/180.
130         last_signal = [self.car.signal1, self.car.signal2, self.car.signal3, orientation, -orientation
131         action = brain.update(last_reward, last_signal)
132         scores.append(brain.score())
133         rotation = action2rotation[action]
134         self.car.move(rotation)
135         distance = np.sqrt((self.car.x - goal_x)**2 + (self.car.y - goal_y)**2)
136         self.ball1.pos = self.car.sensor1
137         self.ball2.pos = self.car.sensor2
138         self.ball3.pos = self.car.sensor3
139
140         if sand[int(self.car.x),int(self.car.y)] > 0:
141             self.car.velocity = Vector(1, 0).rotate(self.car.angle)
142             last_reward = -1
143         else: # otherwise
144             self.car.velocity = Vector(6, 0).rotate(self.car.angle)
145             last_reward = -0.2
```

210

```
Python 2.7.13 |Anaconda 4.3.1 (x86_64)| (default, Dec 20
2016, 23:05:08)
Type "copyright", "credits" or "license" for more
information.

IPython 5.1.0 -- An enhanced Interactive Python.
?          -> Introduction and overview of IPython's features.
%quickref -> Quick reference.
help       -> Python's own help system.
object?    -> Details about 'object', use 'object??' for extra
details.

Restarting kernel...



In [1]:
```

Action equals brain update less reward less signal less
signal will be the input of the neural network. You know
it's composed of the three signals of the sensors Plus the
orientation and minus orientation. So that's the inputs
but then the output is the action to play. And that's only
what we'll be taking from our AI I felt that we're about to
make. So keep that in mind. It's very simple. We first
import the decriminalization from the AI AI then we

create the object brain from the human class which takes as inputs the encoded vectors for the states of five dimensions the three signals plus orientation plus minus orientation. Reactions go left, go straight or go right. And then this gamma parameter. That's the only parameters of the class that we'll be making. And then once we create that object we select in the game class the action to play at each time. And that depends on the last word. And the Lusignan which is the input and that's all that's the only purpose of making this say that in order to have a real artificial intelligence playing the right actions then each time the right move instead of having random actions like we observed in the previous project. All right, so let's do this. Let's implement our artificial intelligence. And as we said we are going to start by importing all the libraries that we'll be using to implement. So that way we will have all the tools we need. All right, so let's start with the first one. The first one is the inevitable non-pay library, the non-Thai library. I always recommend importing it. It's the library which allows us to play and work with the Iraqis. And this here is just a shortcut for more convenience when we want to use numbers. All right then the second library is random. So this is just because we will be taking some random samples from different batches when implementing experience replay. So we have to import this random library as well. Then we will import os that will be just useful when we want to load the model because you know once the model is ready we will implement some code to save the model and then another code to load the model. That's when we want to you know save the brain and load the brain whenever you want to shut down your computer and we use the brain that was trained before for some new experiment. So that's important. Then we are going to import the torch library essential. That's because we will be implementing our neural network with my torch which I recommend much more than the other ones for artificial intelligence because it can handle dynamic graphs. So there we go with torche then from torche we are going to import torche start and end the end module is the most essential one that's the module that contains all the tools to implement some neural networks. And of course there will be a deep neural network that will take as inputs the three signals of the three sensors plus orientation and minus orientation and will return as output the action to play. Well actually to return the q values of the different actions and using a soft Max. We will return the action to play only one the most relevant one to accomplish the cards go to torture and in most essential one then we are going to give a short cut to the functional package. From here we go with the functional package from the end and Maggio. So this functional package contains the different functions that we use when implementing a neural network. So typically the last function we will be using the Google loss because that improves convergence and the loss is contained in this functional submodule from the end module. And since all this is pretty long we're going to give it a shortcut and we're going to call it f simply. Then only 3 modules to import left. So the next one is another central one which is up to him and we take it from still the torture library and then up there we go and let's just call it up to him instead of torture atom. That's of course for the optimizer. We will be importing some optimizers to perform C-grade in the sense so we will definitely need it and then we need to import autographs. And that's only to take the variable class from our regret. So the purpose of it is a little bit technical. Basically we need to import the variable class to make some conversion from tensors which are like more advanced arrays to avoid all that contains a gradient.

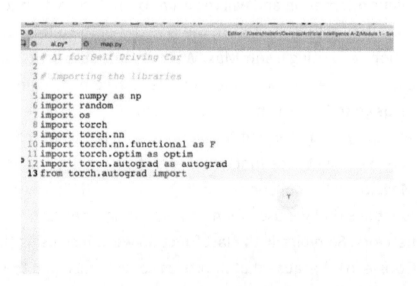

```
1 # AI for Self Driving Car
2
3 # Importing the libraries
4
5 import numpy as np
6 import random
7 import os
8 import torch
9 import torch.nn
10 import torch.nn.functional as F
11 import torch.optim as optim
12 import torch.autograd as autograd
13 from torch.autograd import
```

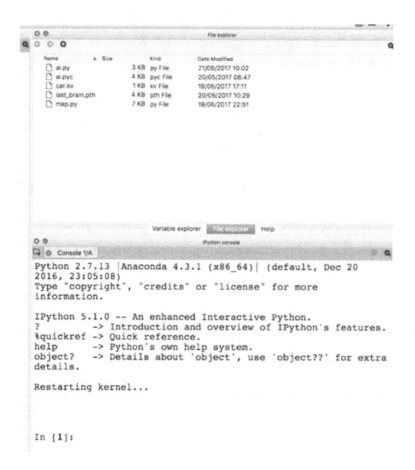

So it's like we don't want to have only a tensor by itself. We want to put the tensor into a variable that will also contain a gradient and to do this we need to use the variable class to convert this tensor into a variable containing the tensor and the gradient. So that's a little bit technical but that's what we have to do when working with PI torch. And we do this thanks to the variable class. But before getting the variable class we need to import torche that grade and let's give a shortcut as well undergrad and then from torch that undergrad we import

215

Roybal There we go. And now we have all the libraries that we'll be using to implement our AI. So we won't bother importing any other library. We have all the tools we need. And now we are ready to create the architecture of the neural network. So that's exactly what we will do in the next project.

SELF DRIVING CAR - STEP 4

All right, so we have very exciting soil ahead of us. We are going to start by creating the architecture of the neural network. That is, we will make the neural network that will be at the heart of our AI and that will return the action to play at age 90. So let's do this. So since we want our neural network to be objective we're going to make it class. And that's because it's much more convenient. You know the class is the model of something we want to build. We want to build a neural network and we need to make some kind of instructions which will all be contained in the class. And in this class we're going to make two functions. First the init function which is the function that comes up all the time when making class. And that basically defines the variable of your object that is the neural network. You know the variables attached to the object as opposed to the global variables. And so this is in this function that will define the architecture of the new network you know, defining the input layer which will be composed of five input neurons because we have five dimensions for the encoded vector of input states.

Then we will define some hidden layers. Maybe you will start with one hidden layer and then you will be welcome to try some other architectures of the neural network. And then of course we will end up with the output layer that will contain the possible actions that we can play at each time. So that's exactly what we'll do in this function. And then we will make another function still inside the class which will be the forward function and that will be the function that will activate the neurons in the neural network. You know this will activate the signals and so we will use a rectified activation function because of course we're dealing with a purely nonlinear problem and this rectified function breaks the linearity. But mostly we're making this Ford function to return the q values which are the outputs of the network. But we have one key value for each action. And later on we'll be returning the final action by either taking the max of the key values or using a soft Max method. We will see that afterwards. So in this project we're going to start by implementing the init function and then the next one will be implementing the forward function. So let's do this. First we need to introduce our class. So we start with class and we give a name to our class which is where we can call it network. And then in this network class I'm going to use an object programming technique which is called inheritance and that is just to inherit from all the tools of a parent class. So our network class that we're about to make is a child test of a larger class which is. And that module. So that's

217

just to inherit from all the tools of this module class which of course are the tools to implement a neural network. So that's a very powerful and evolution trick in object oriented programming that's going heritance. And right now we are inheriting from this module parent class. All right and now we're ready to go inside the class. So I'm pressing enter twice actually because we'll be making two functions and we're starting with the end function. So the init function we have to name it this way with two on this course then in it. And then again to underscore that's just Python syntax, that is just how we have to do it. And then we need to put the arguments. So we have three arguments. The first one is a compulsory argument that is actually self and Self. There is no mystery about it that refers to the object that will be created from this class that we're about to make.

```
1 # AI for Self Driving Car
2
3 # Importing the libraries
4
5 import numpy as np
6 import random
7 import os
8 import torch
9 import torch.nn as nn
10 import torch.nn.functional as F
11 import torch.optim as optim
12 import torch.autograd as autograd
13 from torch.autograd import Variable
14
15 # Creating the architecture of the Neural Network
16
17 class Network(nn.Module):
18
19     def __init__(self, input_size, nb_action):
20         super(Network, self).__init__()
21         self.input_size = input_size
22         self.nb_action = nb_action
23         self.fc1 = nn.Linear(input_size, 30)
24         self.fc2 = nn.Linear(30, nb_action)
```

```
Python 2.7.13 |Anaconda 4.3.1 (x86_64)| (default, Dec 20
2016, 23:05:08)
Type "copyright", "credits" or "license" for more
information.

IPython 5.1.0 -- An enhanced Interactive Python.
?         -> Introduction and overview of IPython's features.
%quickref -> Quick reference.
help      -> Python's own help system.
object?   -> Details about 'object', use 'object??' for extra
details.

Restarting kernel...


In [1]:
```

You know we're making this class. It's like some
instruction on some model of this neural network we
want to build. And then once the class is ready we can
make as many with networks as we want. And each of
these new networks will be some object of this class and
since we will be using the object for some other purposes
we need to know what the variables of the object are and
to Spudis we're using this self here to specify that we're
referring to the object. So whenever I want to use
available from my object I will use self before the variable

to specify that this is a variable of the object. All right so that's the first argument and then we have two other arguments which are of course the number of input neurons and the number of output neurons. So the number of input neurons we're going to call it input size and that's actually five because our input vectors have five dimensions to three signals plus orientation plus minus orientation that are vectors of encoded values that describe one state of the environment. These five values are enough to describe the state of the environment. We could have thought of Less values or more values but that's what I tried and it actually makes sense because we actually need one signal from the left one in front of us and one at the right. You know when we're driving a car we could have gone for a 360 signal you know like the signals at the top of the Google cars that we can totally self-drive with three sensors and then we have this orientation and minus orientation to you know keep track of the goal that you were trying to reach. And then we have of course the output neurons of our network which correspond to the actions and we have three possible actions going left, going straight or going right. And therefore I'm going to call it and the action and there will be three of them. All right. So far we only have to give names to the inputs and then we'll use these volleyballs to do the conditions inside the neural network. All right then and you start by using another torch trick. This trick is a superfunction that's a function that actually inherits from the module. So that's why we had to use inheritance to inherit the module too. This is the first to use. And so basically we're only using this super trick superfunction to be able to use the tools of the module that's much more efficient. And inside the superfunction I just need to specify first the network. So that's our network chul class you know because this is inheriting from the module parent class and then our object. And then I'm just adding that and are in a function like this exactly how we named it. All right so that's just a trick that's just to use all the tools I have. And in that module then we can move on to the next step which is to specify the input layer. So basically what I have to do is introduce a new variable that will be attached to the object and this variable will contain the number of input neurons. So not to be confused with input size input size is the argument of the end function. But that's not the variable that is attached to the object yet the variable that is attached to the object. Well as I just mentioned we need to specify that it is instead attached to the object so we use a self taught and now we give a name to this first variable attached to the object. And so we can simply give the same name as the input. We can call it input size and we will say it is equal to the arguments of a function that is input size. All right. Each time I'm creating an object from the network class and I'm specifying the input size like for example I'm putting 5. There will be 5 here and therefore the input size variable of our object will have the value of 5 because this input size here will be 5 and therefore our new network will have 5 input neurons in the input layer. All right. And then that's the same for the other variable that we want to attach to objects. And as you might have guessed this is going to be a variable for the number of output neurons. And to say we take our object self and then we give a name to this second variable of the object we are going to call it and the action. And this will be equal to this argument here given the number of actions that is the number of output neurons. And so we set it equal to the action actually and the action will be equal to three. Therefore the variable and the action attached to our object to a network will get the value of three. Actually we can see warning here it says undefined name. And then well that's because here we use the. And then shortcut. And we need to use a shortcut here. And for our torche start and in Mudgal and then it will disappear. Here we go. Perfect. Right now we have new warnings all the warnings here are just to specify that what we import is not yet used. That's ok we will be using them afterwards. All right then we have another two variables we want to define for object. And this will be the full connections the full connections between the different layers of our neural network. So since right now we want to make a neural network composed of only one head in their world there will be two full connections. There will be one first full connection between the input layer and the hidden layer. And one second full connection between the hill there and the output layer. So let's start with the first full connection. We're going to call it SE1 And again I use self here to specify that FC one is a variable of my object to solve that. FC one which will be equal to. And now we use the N in module and we're going to use a function called linear R and that's exactly to make this full connection between the neurons and the input layer to the neurons of the hidden there. And what do I mean by full connection. That means that all the neurons of the input layer will all be connected to all the neurons of the Here in there. And so to make this connection we use this linear function to which we need to put some arguments. And as you can see these arguments are in features. So that is the number of neurons of the first law you want to connect them out features that is the number of neurons of the second layer you want to connect that is the layer at the right that is the hidden layer and bicycle's true. So it's true we will keep the default value that's in order to have a bias and not only some weight attached to the run we'll have to wait and one bias for each layer. And so well let's see what we need to input. So the first argument in features is the number of input neurons in the input layer. And so where is it? Well that's actually imprecise. That's the argument of our init function which later we'll be able to fight the three signals orientation and Mannus orientation. So here we go. When the first arguments and put size and then the second argument are out features that is the number of neurons we want to have in the second layer. The second layer that will be fully connected to the first layer. And so now the question is how many neurons do we want in this hidden layer. Well I did a lot of parameter training. I did a lot of experimenting. That's what we do or that's what we do deeper. In general we do a lot of experimenting to see what would be the best neural network for our specific problem. And so I tried many values and I ended up choosing 30 30 runs in a hidden layer and you will see that with this number we will get some pretty good results but then feel free to change the architecture of the neural network. Feel free to play with it. You can not only change the number of neurons in the here and there but also you can add some more layers so that maybe you get an even better car but 30 hinna neurons will get us a good neural network and a good cause. So that's what we go for. And there we go. We have our first full connection really with this linear function. We make the connection between the input layer and the hidden leg. And now time to make the second full connection that is the full connection between the hidden layer and the output layer. So there we go. We're going to call this second full connection at C2. There we go. And still this is available for more objects using Saphir. And then again we use. Well actually we can copy this because we're going to use the N in the module and then the linear function. But then we need to change the arguments of course first.

That's the same first is the number of neurons we're going to have in the first layer of the connection. So that's hidden there. And therefore that is 30 and then the second argument is the number of neurons in the second layer of the connection and that corresponds to the output layer and the output there is. And the actual neurons which later will be three because we have three possible actions but so far we have to use the names we defined. That is the name of the argument of the init function and therefore we input here and the action and there we go. First of all our tuple connections are. And second of all are any functions of Israel. So that's what we'll initialize our object whenever we create an object from the network class. And so as soon as we create an object well all these variables for variables here input size and reaction. You an and two will be defined. And that's how we'll get the architecture of our animal network for each object that we create. Each object will correspond to a neural network of five input neurons, 30 hidden neurons and three output neurons. So there we go. We are done with this first function and now we can move on to the second function which is the forward function and that will be used to activate the neurons in the neural network using the rectifier activation function and mostly to eventually return to cube values which are the outputs of only one network.

SELF DRIVING CAR - STEP 5

All right so we just build the architecture of a neural network with the function of our network class and then we're going to make a second function which is going to be the forward function and that's the function that will activate the neurons. That is the function that will perform for propagation. So let's do this, let's make this function, let's call it forward as we just said and this function is going to take two arguments. First is as usual you know to be able to use the variables of the object because we're going to use SE1 NFC too. So we need the self to be able to use these variables and then we're going to need a second argument which is our input and we're going to call it state because state is exactly the input of our neural networks. You know that's the States. There are other inputs entering the neural network and then outputs will have the q values of the three possible actions: go left , go straight or go right. But we don't need to put it as an argument here because that's exactly what we want to return to this forward function is not only going to activate the neurons but also and mostly it will return the cube values for each possible action depending on the input state here. All right. So that's the two arguments we need. And now let's go inside the function and let's specify what we wanted to do. OK so the first thing we're going to do is activate the hidden neurons and we're going to call the hidden neurons by the variable x so x represents the hidden neurons. And so how to activate them. Well of course we're going to take our input neurons. We're going to use our first full connection if you want to get the hidden neurons and then we're going to apply an inactivation function on them which will be the rectified function. So how are you going to do that? Remember we imported the torch. And it's that functional module that contains all the functions in order to implement the neural network. And we gave it the shortcut. So actually what we're going to do now is we're going to use one of these functions from the functional module and this function is to really function. So what is really relevant is the rectifier function that you saw in the intuition lectures. That's just and then given to the rectifier function. But since this function is taken from and in that function which was given the shortcut we need to type here first of thoughts and then that's where we can take this function. And actually if I type are we here we go we have the real function. So that's directed by a function that will activate the hidden neurons that are x. So in this real function now we understand perfectly what we have to input, that's the neurons that we want to activate. That is the hidden neurons and so to get these hidden neurons we are going to take our first full connection one which we will apply to our input neurons to go from the input neurons to the neurons. So let's take our first full connection. But our first full connection is a variable of our object. Therefore we need

228

to type here first. FC one here we go. That's the first full connection of our neural network. And inside this personal connection we are going to input our output states to go from the input neurons to the hidden neurons. And so since we gave it the name STATE Well here we have two input states and there we go. We now get activated hidden neurons. All right. And now that we have the hidden neurons we are going to return the output neurons. So next line and as you understood the output neurons correspond to our actions. But these are not the actions directly.

```python
1 # AI for Self Driving Car
2
3 # Importing the libraries
4
5 import numpy as np
6 import random
7 import os
8 import torch
9 import torch.nn as nn
10 import torch.nn.functional as F
11 import torch.optim as optim
12 import torch.autograd as autograd
13 from torch.autograd import Variable
14
15 # Creating the architecture of the Neural Network
16
17 class Network(nn.Module):
18
19     def __init__(self, input_size, nb_action):
20         super(Network, self).__init__()
21         self.input_size = input_size
22         self.nb_action = nb_action
23         self.fc1 = nn.Linear(input_size,  )
24         self.fc2 = nn.Linear(30, nb_action)
25
26     def forward(self, state):
27         x = F.relu(self.fc1(state))
28         q_values = self.fc2(x)
29         return q_values
```

Python 2.7.13 |Anaconda 4.3.1 (x86_64)| (default, Dec 20
2016, 23:05:08)
Type "copyright", "credits" or "license" for more
information.

IPython 5.1.0 -- An enhanced Interactive Python.
?   -> Introduction and overview of IPython's features.
%quickref -> Quick reference.
help   -> Python's own help system.
object?   -> Details about 'object', use 'object??' for extra
details.

Restarting kernel...

These are the q values because we're building a digital model that combines a deeper model to Q learning and therefore we use q learning here to get the q values for each of our actions and then later using soughed Max or in our Max we will get the final action so here the Voivode I'm about to introduce will correspond to the APA nuance and since the output neurons are the key values. Well I'm going to call this variable. Q That means that we go to q values and now we directly take our food connection which is the variable. To put a variable from our object. So we take here self taught F C to and of course here we input the neurons of the left side of this connection. That is what we got from the first line which is x. So x There we go. We now get our Q values. That's the output neurons of our neural network. OK. And then the last line of code of course this forward function is used to return these values. So we just have to add a return and simply Q values and that will return the key values for each possible action: go left , go straight or go right. All right. So congratulations. We're done with our first class and actually we were done making the architecture of the neural network. Remember this is not a finished job. You can always improve the architecture of the neural network by trying different ones. So feel free to do that by adding more neurons here. For example if you want to add 50 hidden neurons you can just replace the 30 here and the 30 here by 50 50 and 50 and then you can add some more hidden layers by making some useful connections. Well that's really the job of an artist. There is no general rule of what would be the best architecture in each situation. So that's why we have to experiment. Let's try with that and you will see that we'll eventually get a pretty good self-driving car. All right. And now we're going to make the next class which is about experience replay and we will be making that in the next three to two hours.

SELF DRIVING CAR - STEP 6

So we're going to make a new class which we will call replay memory and that will implement experience to play exactly as you saw in the intuition lectures. But first let's give a quick reminder about what is experience replay. So you know all this artificial intelligence is based on Markov decision processes and Markov decision processes consist of looking at a series of events. So events are you know for example going from one state to the next state and tipis one. But if events were like that well since the next day it is very correlated to the current state. Well the network would not be doing very well. So for those coming from the deep learning course that's exactly the same as where we learned our time series with only one timestep. It was not learning anything because one timestep was not sufficient enough for a model to learn to understand long term correlations. So that's the same here and that's why we have to implement the experience replay. So how does it work? Well that's very simple instead of only considering the current state that is only one state at time t. We're going to consider more in the past. So exactly like for lithiums and therefore our series of events will not be as. And I suppose one this will be for example the one hundred states in the past. So as T-minus one hundred eighty minus 99 up to as minus 1 and then S-T. So in other words we put 100 less transitions into what we call the memory and that's why we have a long term memory as opposed to a short term memory or even should I say an instant memory and that makes the whole process work much better. And then once we create this memory of the last 100 events we will simply say that it will take some random batches of these transitions to make our next update. That is our next move by selecting the next section and therefore in this replay memory class that we're implementing for experience replay we will make three functions. First of all the function as usual that's the case for any class. And so in this function we will define the variables that will be attached to the future instances of the class, that is the future objects that will be created from this class. And so very simply these variables will be the memory of the 100 transitions to 100 events. And the capacity that is the 100 number you will be welcome to try a longer memory by increasing the capacity. So that's the first function in it and then we'll make two other functions, one push function to make sure that the memory doesn't ever contain more than 100 transitions. And for this we'll use the capacity by just doing one simple condition and then eventually we will make the simple function and that will be of course to sample some transitions in this memory of the last 100 transitions. All right, so let's start by introducing the class. So as you know we start with class and then we give them to the class we call it replay memory and then in parenthesis we input an object then Cullin and then we go we start with the first function. The end is a function. So that's exactly the same as before we start with death. Then two underscores in it two underscores again and then the variables. So there is of course self which is the variable attached to the future instances of the class of future objects and then we're going to have another variable for you to be able to try some other experience with some of the memories and that's going to be the capacity. So this capacity will simply be the number one hundred because we're going to make experience playing with one hundred less transitions.

```python
1 # AI for Self Driving Car
2
3 # Importing the libraries
4
5 import numpy as np
6 import random
7 import os
8 import torch
9 import torch.nn as nn
10 import torch.nn.functional as F
11 import torch.optim as optim
12 import torch.autograd as autograd
13 from torch.autograd import Variable
14
15 # Creating the architecture of the Neural Network
16
17 class Network(nn.Module):
18
19     def __init__(self, input_size, nb_action):
20         super(Network, self).__init__()
21         self.input_size = input_size
22         self.nb_action = nb_action
23         self.fc1 = nn.Linear(input_size, 30)
24         self.fc2 = nn.Linear(30, nb_action)
25
26     def forward(self, state):
27         x = F.relu(self.fc1(state))
28         q_values = self.fc2(x)
29         return q_values
30
31 # Implementing Experience Replay
32
33 class ReplayMemory(object):
34
35     def __init__(self, capacity):
36         self.capacity = capacity
37         self.memory = []
```

```
Name              ▲ Size        Kind          Date Modified
□ ai.py             3 KB        py File       21/05/2017 10:02
□ ai.pyc            4 KB        pyc File      20/05/2017 08:47
□ car.kv            1 KB        kv File       19/06/2017 17:11
□ last_brain.pth    4 KB        pth File      20/05/2017 10:29
□ map.py            7 KB        py File       19/06/2017 22:51
```

Variable explorer   File explorer   Help

Console 1/A

```
Python 2.7.13 |Anaconda 4.3.1 (x86_64)| (default, Dec 20
2016, 23:05:08)
Type "copyright", "credits" or "license" for more
information.

IPython 5.1.0 -- An enhanced Interactive Python.
?          -> Introduction and overview of IPython's features.
%quickref -> Quick reference.
help       -> Python's own help system.
object?    -> Details about 'object', use 'object??' for extra
details.

Restarting kernel...


In [1]:
```

All right and then Collon And here we go. Let's go inside the function and let's define the variables of our replay memory object. So the first one will be a self taught capacity and as you probably understood this will be the capacity that is the maximum number of transitions we want to have in our memory of events. And this will be equal to the arguments who will input when creating an object of the replay memory class and therefore that is capacity. That's the argument of the init function. So capacity. So again not to be confused with self that capacity is the name of the variable that is attached to the object and capacity here is the argument who will input when creating an object of the replay memory class. All right. And then we have a second voice. That's of course the memory. So self taught Nemec. All right. And so what will this memory Voivode be ? Well this memory is supposed to contain the last 100 events and therefore this should be a simple test. You know a list which will contain the last 100 events, the last 100 transitions and to initialize the list. There is nothing more simple, we just add some brackets like that. And here we go. Our memory is initialized so of course at the beginning of the experiment or more precisely the beginning of the exploration the memory will be an empty list and then we will put the transitions. Each time we reach a future state. And speaking of that, that's exactly what we will do with the next function that we're going to call the push function. We will make this push function to plant the events in this memory list and then we'll use the capacity to make sure that this memory list always contains 100 events and never more.

SELF DRIVING CAR - STEP 7

All right now we're going to make the push function which will do two tasks. First it will depend on a new transition or a new event in the memory and then second it will make sure that the memory always has 100 transitions. I'm seeing 100 because we gave the example of 100 events in the previous project but in fact this will be much more than 100. This will be rather maybe ten thousand one hundred thousand we'll see. But anyway this value will be the capacity. All right. So let's make this push function. So as usual we start with death to define a new function and then we give a name to this function so we call it push and this function will have two arguments. First as usual self that refers to the object and the next one. Why do you think that will be? Well remember this push function will be used to append a new event into memory. We already have the memory. So what we need now is a variable is an event that will be our arguments or input and we will bend this input into memory which is a variable of the object. All right. So you can actually call it an event or transition. That's the same and you will see in the next code sections. What exactly is this event? What form it has. Actually I can tell you now this event, this transition that we're adding to the memory is a total of four elements. The first one is the last state that is etsy. The second one is the new state of Estep. The third one is the last section that is 80. The action that was displayed

238

and the fourth one is the last word the last word
obtained. That is our. So that's exactly the form that this
event will have.

```python
# AI for Self Driving Car

# Importing the libraries

import numpy as np
import random
import os
import torch
import torch.nn as nn
import torch.nn.functional as F
import torch.optim as optim
import torch.autograd as autograd
from torch.autograd import Variable

# Creating the architecture of the Neural Network

class Network(nn.Module):

    def __init__(self, input_size, nb_action):
        super(Network, self).__init__()
        self.input_size = input_size
        self.nb_action = nb_action
        self.fc1 = nn.Linear(input_size, 30)
        self.fc2 = nn.Linear(30, nb_action)

    def forward(self, state):
        x = F.relu(self.fc1(state))
        q_values = self.fc2(x)
        return q_values

# Implementing Experience Replay

class ReplayMemory(object):

    def __init__(self, capacity):
        self.capacity = capacity
        self.memory = []

    def push(self, event):
        self.memory.append(event)
        if len(self.memory) > self.capacity:
            del self.memory[0]
```

All right. And that's all we just need the event because we just want to pin the event to the memory and then make sure that the memory has capacity elements. All right so now let's go inside the function. So the first thing we'll do is attend to you then to the memory. And that's very simple because we're going to use the append function. So that will be direct. And when we use the append function we must start with the list to which we want to spend something and this list is of course memory. So we start with memory and since memory is a variable of the object we start here with self taught memory that we go to set up memory and then we have to do that and then the open function which is the first one. So it bent and inside the open function we input what we want to spend to memory which is of course our evidence. So even here. And that will append the new event composed of the last eight new states, last action and last word to the memory. All right. So that's the first thing done. And then the second thing we need to do is make sure that the memory always contains capacity elements. So let's say capacity is now 100000. That's probably the capacity you will choose because then one million elements might make the train slow. So let's say 100000. Now we're going to make sure that our memory always contains 100000 transitions, 100000 events and never more. So of course at the beginning it will have one then two and three but then once it reaches 100000 events Well it will always have 100000 events. So to make sure of it we simply need to make an IF condition with this upper bound that we don't want to go over. So if we get the idea that we'll use here is that if we go over the limit Well we will delete the first transition the first event of the memory and therefore we're going to take the lead function to take the length of the memory that is the number of elements in the memory. So here in the len function we can put self memory to memory. So if the number of elements of that memory is larger than the capacity well in that case we will remove the first element to make sure that the memory always has the same number of capacity elements and to do the first element there is nothing more simple we are going to use another function which is the tell byte centric so well and therefore we want to remove the first transition which is the oldest transition in the memory because the last transitions are the ones that we are tense and therefore that's the new transitions. So the first transitions are the oldest ones. And so here we want to delete self taught memory and records and we take the first element of the memory which has an zero itself that memory zero Now interesting I have a little warning which says that there is an undefined capacity. That's because the capacity here is not the input that must be the capacity variable attached to the object and therefore you will need to add a self self that capacity. And now the warning has come. Now you understand even more the use of self that's really to refer to the object to take the capacity of the object that will be created, that is an instance of the replay memory class. All right. So we're done with this push function. And so now we can move on to the next function which is the simple function which will take some random samples from this memory at the last capacity elements and doing this will improve a lot. The deep cleaning process.

SELF DRIVING CAR - STEP 8

All right we have one last function to implement in our replay memory class. That's the simple function and that's of course to get some random samples from our memory. And therefore this function will return these random samples. All right, so let's get into it. We are going to call it simple. Here we go. And this function takes two arguments as input. The first one as usual self our future object to replay memory class and the second argument is can you try to guess. Well we're taking some samples of fixed size and therefore we need to choose a size for samples and more precisely we call it a batch size. So that's the name we're going to give to our second argument batch size. And there we go. We have our two arguments and now we can implement the simple function. So now I just want to warn you this is going to get a little technical but I'll try my best to explain. So we're going to start by creating the sample variable. This is just the variable that will contain the samples of the memory. All right, so simple is equal. And so now how are we going to get these samples? Well first of all we have to take our memory because we are getting the samples from our memory. Then we will probably need the batch size because the samples are going to contain batch size Elon's. So we need memory, we need batch size and then we need some torche or bison tricks to get a good format of these samples. So what I'm going to do I'm going to write the line of code and then I'm going to explain that element by element. So let's do it. I'm starting by taking a zip function. I'm going to explain very soon what it does. And inside this function I'm going to add a star. I'm going to expand that as well. The Star and random thought Central so random as you might have guessed is the random library that we imported here. So that's the main reason why we had to import these random libraries because we're taking some random samples. So from this random library we're going to use the simple function. So this is our variables and this is a function so I'm going to add some parenthesis. And now as you can see the sample is a function and we have to put some arguments so that you can see the first argument itself. And actually speaking of self this corresponds to self-talk memory, the memory of our future instance object of our replay memory for us. So I'm going to add that memory here and then the second argument is as you might have guessed, the size of the Bechuana taken randomly from our memory and that we gave it a name that is batch size. So the second argument is going to be Bachche sucks. All right. So the line of code is typed and I'm going to explain what it does. So first of all with this random dot simple function we are taking some random samples from the memory that had a fixed size of that size. So that's understandable. But then what does this Zipp star function do? Well there is no mystery about it. It is just like a reshape function. So for example I'm going to add a

244

little come here just to explain that I'm going to remove it. So let's say that for example we have a list of the following elements for example. First one two three. And then the second element. Four five six. So we have a list of two doubles of three elements one two three four five six. Well then if I apply the zip function with the star on it. Well what would become so Zip star list is going to be equal to a new list but of a different shape and different shape is going to be one for then two three and then five six. All right. So that's just what it does. It just reshapes your list. OK so now that you understand what this Zipp star list does. Well now let's explain why we had to do it. So as you understood we are going to add the events to the memory and the events have the form. First the state, then the action and then the reward. But for our algorithm we don't want this format, we actually want our samples to have the following format. A format is composed of three samples: one sample for the states, one sample for the actions and one sample for the reward. So for example let's say that this one to three is state one action one. We want one and then state to action two and we were to well what we want is one batch for each one batch for state one and state two. One is a match for action one in action two and a third that for we were one and we were two. That's just the format that is going to be expected next because then we'll wrap these batches into a pie towards horrible impact which far we will remember is a variable that contains both a tensor and a gradient. And that in order to be able to differentiate with respect to a tensor to be able to differentiate with respect to intenser within the structure of a horrible containing tensor and a gradient. Again that's how the Pi torch works. So to summarize we create one batch for each of the state's actions and rewards and then we're going to put each of these vets separately into some bytes which Horrible's which each one will get a gradient so that eventually we'll be able to differentiate each of them. All right so that's the purpose of the Zipp function. So let me just remove this comment. And now the only thing that we have to do is to return the samples. So as I just explained we cannot return the samples directly for the simple reason that we want to put the samples into a by torche viable. So to do this for each of the samples we're going to use the map function and this map function will do the mapping from the samples to torture variables that will contain a tensor and a gradient. So as you can see this map function takes several arguments. The first argument is a function and this function is going to be the function that will convert the samples into some torche variables. And the second argument is what we want to apply this function onto. So that will be the arguments of this function and therefore what is it going to be. That's of course going to be the samples. So the second argument here is going to be the symbols. But then let's define the function on which we want to apply. Each of the symbols. So to define a function here we need to first give a name to the function which will be called lambda. That's just a name and giving Lenda then X which is going to be the variable of this function. So that is just a name and giving for the variable and then. And here we give the expression of the function that is what we want this lambda function to return and see what it is going to be. It's supposed to be something that will convert our samples into a torch variable and to do this. We already mentioned it in some previous projects. Well we have the Voivode function for them. The Voice will function. We'll make that conversion from a torch dancer to a variable that will contain the sensor and the greatest. So the first thing I'm going to add here is a variable inside of which I'm going to convert X because X is going to be the simplest ones that will be applied onto the samples. But then that's all there is one last technical thing that we need to implement is the fact that for each batch which is contained in the sample for example the batch of actions a 1 8 2 3 and the other actions we have to concatenate it with respect to the first time engine which corresponds to the States. And why do we have to make this concatenation? It's just for everything to be well aligned. That is that in each row to state the action and the reward corresponds to the same time t..

```python
1 # AI for Self Driving Car
2
3 # Importing the libraries
4
5 import numpy as np
6 import random
7 import os
8 import torch
9 import torch.nn as nn
10 import torch.nn.functional as F
11 import torch.optim as optim
12 import torch.autograd as autograd
13 from torch.autograd import Variable
14
15 # Creating the architecture of the Neural Network
16
17 class Network(nn.Module):
18
19     def __init__(self, input_size, nb_action):
20         super(Network, self).__init__()
21         self.input_size = input_size
22         self.nb_action = nb_action
23         self.fc1 = nn.Linear(input_size, 30)
24         self.fc2 = nn.Linear(30, nb_action)
25
26     def forward(self, state):
27         x = F.relu(self.fc1(state))
28         q_values = self.fc2(x)
29         return q_values
30
31 # Implementing Experience Replay
32
33 class ReplayMemory(object):
34
35     def __init__(self, capacity):
36         self.capacity = capacity
37         self.memory = []
38
39     def push(self, event):
40         self.memory.append(event)
41         if len(self.memory) > self.capacity:
42             del self.memory[0]
43
44     def sample(self, batch_size):
45         samples = zip(*random.sample(self.memory, batch_size))
46         return map(lambda x: Variable(torch.cat(x, 0)), samples)
```

248

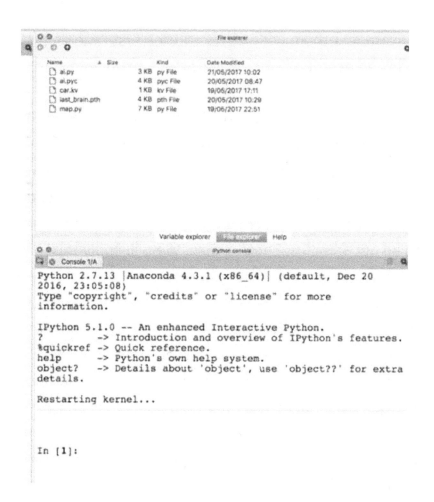

So that eventually we get a list of batches all well-aligned and each batch is a pie towards Voivod. So how can we make this concatenation? Well we need to use the cat function from the torch library. So we're going to add a torch to which we add that gets applied to X but then in this function we need to specify the dimension with respect to which we want to make that concatenation. And as I just mentioned this is the first time an engine has been indexed. And here we go we have our function ready this Lunda that function will take the samples concatenate them with respect to the first time engine and then eventually we convert the sensors into some torche variables that contains both a tensor and a gradient so that later when we apply to castigate in the sense we will be able to differentiate to have data weights. All right so this function is ready. And then here is the second argument of the map function. We need to specify what we want to apply to this function and that is on all our samples. There we go. We will apply this lambda function on all the samples so that eventually we obtain a list of matches where each match is a PI torch viable. All right so that was quite technical but now at least everything will work well. We want to use this technique. Afterwards we only use it here so if you don't want to have a deep understanding of the technical details here well that's fine you can just copy these three lines of code to simplify your memory if you want to make an artificial intelligence by torch it as you want. But now the good news is that we're done with this replaying memory class experience replay is now implemented and we can move on to the next and final class which will be the whole security mode. So in this model we will have of course our network who will experience replay and then all the rest of the security algorithm. So it's going to be a much bigger class. We're going to make about 10 functions but that's only because we're doing this step by step so that you can better understand what's going on.

SELF DRIVING CAR - STEP 9

We are going to make the first step into implementing the deep theory model. So basically we are about to implement the whole process of the diffusion algorithm. And so we are going to use what we created before. That is the architecture of the neural network to replay memory to integrate this into the whole dequeue learning process. And this whole learning algorithm is going to fit into one class. That's the last that we're making to implement artificial intelligence. And this class will just contain different functions. So we will have the functions which will create and initialize all the variables attached to our future detouring objects which will represent the model itself and they will have some other functions. One of them will of course be to select the right action at each time. We will also have an update function core function to get this core and have an idea of how the learning is going if it's going well. If the exploration is going well and if it can move on to exploitation, then we'll have a safe function to save tomorrow that is to save the brain of the car and then eventually load function. So we have a couple of functions to make. We're going to make one function for each to toil. And today we're going to start with the end function as usual when we're making a class. But first let's not forget to introduce the class so we're going to call it D. Q And for your network then some parenthesis call in. And then we go with our first function. So let's do this def then double underscore then its double underscore again and parenthesis. So as you understood in this function we are going to introduce the variables attached to our object. So we are going to have a couple of lines starting all by themselves and we'll basically create and initialize all the variables that are needed to implement the D2 network. So we will for example create an object or network because of course we need our deep neural network then we will need our memory. We will create another variable for the memory. So we'll have another variable self up memory but then that's not all we will have to create as well. Some variables for the last date. The last action and the last word. That's of course you know the variables that you see in the diffusion algorithm. And then what else. Well we will also need an optimizer you know to perform a stochastic grid in the sense of data weights according to how much they will contribute to the error. When the AI is making a mistake and then I think that so that's basically the variables we now need to create and initialize. But in this init function we will put a couple of arguments first as usual self which is the arguments referring to our object. Then since you know we're going to create an object of the network class. Well since the network class takes as argument in the init function input size and the action Well that's the same here. When creating an object of the network class we will need to choose an input size argument and the actual argument. Therefore we can just copy some of them here and there. So these arguments will now become. Also some arguments didn't last. Whenever we create some future objects of the different class that some future dical role models Well we will need to specify the input size which I remind is the number of dimensions in the vectors that are including your states. Your input states and a number of actions which is the number of possible actions the car can make. So I remind you. These can either go left, go straight or go right. Okay, perfect. Then you know you will be creating a new object of the replay memory class to create the memory object to get our memory of the transitions and in the information we have the capacity argument. But since we will only be using it once actually when we create memory and not any thereafter Well we won't need to specify the capacity argument. We could do this but will directly input the number of transitions we want our memory to have. But then we need one last argument which is to get the parameter in the teacher model. Remember this gamma parameter is the delay. And that's a parameter of the equation and therefore we will put it here because we will be using it afterwards several times. So let's put it here. We're going to call it Gamma. So for that it's just the name of the argument and then we go to all the arguments you will need for this in its function. So that means that whenever we create our dictionary model that is whenever we create an object of the teacher in class. Well we will need to specify as arguments the input size, the number of actions and the parameter. And we'll end with the real values for them. All right so now let's go inside the function. OK. So now basically this is going to be easy. We are just about to create and initialize all the variables that we need. And so let's start with the first one. Let's start with gamma. Actually the delay coefficient. So since this is a Voivode wanting to be attached to her object we start with self. So gamma is going to be a variable of our teacher and model itself that gamma equals the arguments that will be input when creating an object of the detune class. So Janna and there we go with the second argument. The second argument is going to be the reward window. So what is this window? Well that's going to be the sliding window of the mean of the last 100 words which you will use just to evaluate the evolution of the performance you know will have the meaning of the word into this war Windu that will slide over time. And what we want to observe is the meaning of the last 100 words increasing with time. So let's initialize it with a self reward underscore window. And so since this is going to be a sliding window of the evolving mean of the last 100 words. Well we're going to initialize it as an empty list and then we will expand to mean that we work overtime. All right, then more exciting. Let's create our neural network. So we're going to call it self-taught Mario because basically that's the heart of the models. I'm calling it model and this model is going to be nothing else than a subject in that class and to create such an object. We take our class network in parenthesis and here we just put the arguments of the class but we put these arguments in the arguments of the init function and therefore we just need to copy them right here and just paste them in the network class and then we go with this line of code. We create one neural network for learning a perfect model then let's create a memory. So again we're going to create a new Vargo that we call self taught memory. And again this is going to be an object of the replay memory class. So let's just take the name or class. Let's copy yet let's face that here and in some parenthesis we need to put the capacity because the capacity is an argument of the function and that's the only argument we need to here. So what capacity are we going to choose, remember that corresponds to the number of transitions, the number of events, the last state you state, the last action and the last word. And so as mentioned in one of the Priester toils we are going to take one hundred thousand one hundred thousand transitions into memory and then we will sample from this memory to get a small number of random transitions and that on which the model will be OK. So now we have our memory perfect. Now let's get our optimizer. So again self we create a new variable that we call optimizer so optimizer is another variable of our future dequeue an object self that optimizer. And now if we go back up you can see that we imported tortured Upton which is a modular torch that contains all the tools to perform to get the grid in the center. So of course it contains some optimizers and we gave it the shortcut Upton and therefore here what we're going to do is take the model up to him which is torch's that up to him and from this module we are going to take one of the optimizers. So as you can see they're all listed here. Many of them are excellent, for example armor's Propp is an excellent optimizer. There is for example highly recommended for a record of neural networks or unsupervised deep learning. But the other one that is excellent and that he will choose is the atom optimizer. That's the one you'll see that with this one will get a good self-driving car. But again you are totally welcome to try other ones you can try the arms prop but for metal we will choose Adam. So I'm pressing enter. And in fact you'll notice there is the capitol here. That's because we're creating an object of the Atom class. This is a class but the object will be an atom optimizer itself. But since this is a class we need to put some arguments, the arguments of the Atom class and the arguments are all the parameters that can customize your and optimizer. So for example that's typically the learning rate, decay or some other parameters. And besides taking all the parameters of Ormeau we will specify a learning rate. So it's the beginning of the parameters of our model. We can get them with a self doubt model. So that's the model we created here, a self-taught model from our own class. So a self-taught model and then to access the parameters of the model we add another dot and then parameters with some parenthesis very simply. So that's just to connect the addon optimizer to our neural network, the one that we created here again, then as we just mentioned we're going to add a learning rate and the argument for this is our. And we will set it equal to a value such that the learning doesn't happen too fast if we get a learning rate too large then the AI AI will learn properly. We want to give our AI some time to explore and learn from its mistakes. You know when we punish it when it's making some mistakes like going onto some sense or getting too close to a wall. Well we want to give some time to learn. We want a way to the neural network to date correctly. And so a good value for the learning rate I ended up with after trying several of them is 0.2 or one. All right and that's all we need to create an optimizer. So basically you're creating an object of the Atom class. Great. And then the last three variables we need are the variables composing our transition events. So that's the last date, the last action and the last word. And so that's basically what we'll create now and we'll just need to initialize them. So let's start with the last date the last date we're going to call it self-taught. Last underscore state and then how are you going to initialize it. Well remember the last date is a vector of 5 dominations, a vector that is encoded in one state of the environment. And as a reminder these five dimensions are the three signals of the three sensors left straight and right and orientation and minus orientation. So this is a vector and intuitive sense. But for a torch it needs to be more than a vector. It actually needs to be a torch tensor. But not only it needs to be a torch sensor but also it needs to have one more dimension that I like to call it fake dimension that corresponds to the batch. And that's because the last eight will be the input of the neural network but when working with me when that works in general whether it is with denser flow carries a torch while the input vectors cannot be a simple vector by itself. It has to be in a batch. The network can only accept a batch of input observations and therefore not only will create a tensor for input state vectors but also we will create this fake dimension corresponding to the batch. So let's do this and let's start by initializing a torch tensor so to do this there is nothing more simple. We take our torche library then dot and then we're going to use the tensor class because as you might have guessed this will create an object of the tensor class that is a tensor object. And in this tensor we need to put an argument which will specify the size of the tensor. You can picture it as an array having one single type. But basically what this will represent now is of course this input state which you can see has a vector and so to specify the number of elements distance must have. Well we need to use of course the input size because the input size is exactly the number of dimensions of our input state vectors. Now I should say tensors. And so what we simply need to input in our tensor class to create a tensor object. Well that's imprecise. And later on input size will be quantified. All right, that's good. That's the first thing done. We just initialized the tensor as it should be. But then remember we need to do another thing we need to create that fake dimension because this is what the network will expect for its inputs and to create this one for examination which by the way has to be the first time engine you know the damage you put into the batch will be the first time I mention this let's say very well.

```python
23          self.fc1 = nn.Linear(input_size, 30)
24          self.fc2 = nn.Linear(30, nb_action)
25
26      def forward(self, state):
27          x = F.relu(self.fc1(state))
28          q_values = self.fc2(x)
29          return q_values
30
31 # Implementing Experience Replay
32
33 class ReplayMemory(object):
34
35      def __init__(self, capacity):
36          self.capacity = capacity
37          self.memory = []
38
39      def push(self, event):
40          self.memory.append(event)
41          if len(self.memory) > self.capacity:
42              del self.memory[0]
43
44      def sample(self, batch_size):
45          samples = zip(*random.sample(self.memory, batch_size))
46          return map(lambda x: Variable(torch.cat(x, 0)), samples)
47
48 # Implementing Deep Q Learning
49
50 class Dqn():
51
52      def __init__(self, input_size, nb_action, gamma):
53          self.gamma = gamma
54          self.reward_window = []
55          self.model = Network(input_size, nb_action)
56          self.memory = ReplayMemory(100000)
57          self.optimizer = optim.Adam(self.model.parameters(), lr = 0.001)
58          self.last_state = torch.Tensor(input_size).unsqueeze(0)
59          self.last_action = 0
60
61
62
63
```

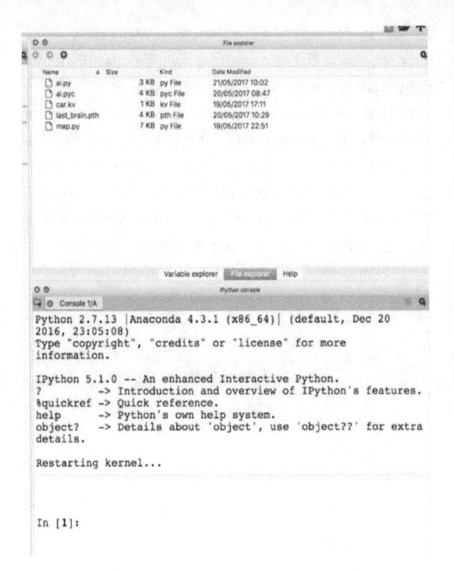

Well to do this we simply need to add that then and squeeze and then in some parenthesis. We need to put the index of this big dimension. And as I just said this fake dimension has to be the first animation of the last date and since indexes and bytes have started zero we need to input zero so that this new paradigm engine is becoming the first line engine. So we have a first time engine corresponding to the batch and then the diamond should respond to that sensor which will contain the five elements of your input states the three signals orientation and minus orientation. And then we went and initialized our input states properly. Perfect. And then two variables to go and that's going to be much easier because the next variable is the last action. That's a new Roybal we are creating for Object last action. And remember in the first project of the section I told you that the actions are going to be either 0 1 or 2 and then using the action rotation vector we will convert these indexes of these actions into the angles of the rotation which I think are 0 20 or minus 20. We can actually refresh our memory with that. Well it is exactly here. Action to rotation if the action is zero. Well this will correspond to the first index of zero if the action is 1. This will correspond to the index one of these vectors of 20 degrees and if the action is to we will get minus 20 degrees that's going to be the rotation angle of our car when we play the action. All right. And therefore since the action is going to be either 0 1 or 2 Well the action is there for a simple number. And so very simply we can initialize it to zero. We don't need to create any tens or hear anything else. We just need to initialize it with zero. And finally. Well that's the last word. It's the self that last word. There we go. And again the word is a float number which I remember is between minus 1 and plus 1. So that's the number again. And as for the action. We will initialize it to zero and then we go. Congratulations if the function is ready. So now we are ready to move on to the exciting stuff. And actually the most important thing for AI that's deciding which action to play at each time and each tanty And that's exactly what we're going to do in the next project by creating the select action method.

SELF DRIVING CAR - STEP 10

In this oil we're going to make a function that will select the right action each time. So basically we're going to implement the part that will make the car the right move. And each time that it's going left going straight or going right to reach the goal and to avoid the obstacles that are descending. So let's do this right now. We are going to start as usual with the deaf to define a function and then we give a name to our function which we're going to call select action then some parenthesis and this select action function will take two arguments. The first one is self as you grow to refer to the object and the second argument which according to you is going to be which one. Well what could it be? If you think about it the action we select comes from the output of the neural network because the output of the neural network or the q values for each of the three possible actions and therefore the action that we play the action that will be the output of the neural network depends on the input state and the input states is exactly the second argument we need with select action function. It's because we're literally going to take the output of the neural network.

```python
31 # Implementing Experience Replay
32
33 class ReplayMemory(object):
34
35     def __init__(self, capacity):
36         self.capacity = capacity
37         self.memory = []
38
39     def push(self, event):
40         self.memory.append(event)
41         if len(self.memory) > self.capacity:
42             del self.memory[0]
43
44     def sample(self, batch_size):
45         samples = zip(*random.sample(self.memory, batch_size))
46         return map(lambda x: Variable(torch.cat(x, 0)), samples)
47
48 # Implementing Deep Q Learning
49
50 class Dqn():
51
52     def __init__(self, input_size, nb_action, gamma):
53         self.gamma = gamma
54         self.reward_window = []
55         self.model = Network(input_size, nb_action)
56         self.memory = ReplayMemory(100000)
57         self.optimizer = optim.Adam(self.model.parameters(), lr = 0.001)
58         self.last_state = torch.Tensor(input_size).unsqueeze(0)
59         self.last_action = 0
60         self.last_reward = 0
61
62     def select_action(self, state):
63         probs = F.softmax(self.model(Variable(state, volatile = True))*7) # T=7
64         action = probs.multinomial()
65         return action.data[0,0]
66
67
68
69
70
71
```

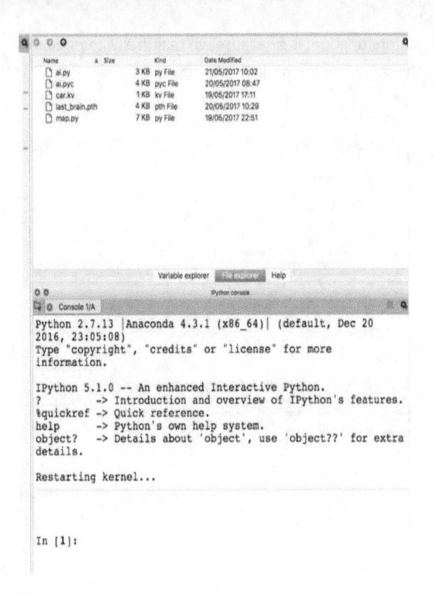

Name	Size	Kind	Date Modified
ai.py	3 KB	py File	21/05/2017 10:02
ai.pyc	4 KB	pyc File	20/05/2017 08:47
car.kv	1 KB	kv File	19/05/2017 17:11
last_brain.pth	4 KB	pth File	20/05/2017 10:29
map.py	7 KB	py File	19/06/2017 22:51

Variable explorer   File explorer   Help

Python console

Console 1/A

Python 2.7.13 |Anaconda 4.3.1 (x86_64)| (default, Dec 20
2016, 23:05:08)
Type "copyright", "credits" or "license" for more
information.

IPython 5.1.0 -- An enhanced Interactive Python.
?   -> Introduction and overview of IPython's features.
%quickref -> Quick reference.
help   -> Python's own help system.
object?   -> Details about 'object', use 'object??' for extra
details.

Restarting kernel...

In [1]:

And of course the output of the neural network directly depends on the input of the neural network. So that's going to be our argument. And now we can give it any name we will actually call it state because the input of the neural networks are the input states that are coded by a vector of five dimensions to three signals orientation and minus orientation. And so now things are going to be easy. We are going to feed the input state into the neural network the one that we build right above right here with the next class and then then we're going to get the outputs which are the key values for each of the three possible actions and then using the soft Max method which I'm going to explain in this project. We're going to get the final action to play. So let's do this, let's go into the function and let's implement all this. So the first thing we need to start with is about what I've just mentioned sighed Max. The idea of the soft Max is that we're going to try to get the best action to play at each time. But at the same time we will be exploring different actions. And how do we do that? How can we get the best action to play while still exploring the other actions? Well we used this idea of stuff which consists of generating a distribution of probabilities for each of the q values. Q States action. Now we have one Q value for each action: go left , go straight or go right. But this q value also depends on the input state. That's exactly the Q function used in intuition lectures. This Q function is a function of the state and the action. So since we have here one input state which is the state here and three possible actions we have three new values Q. State action 1 Q state action 2 and two states action 3 and we are going to generate a distribution of probabilities with respect to these three key values. That is we're going to have one probability for the first Q value, one probability for the second Q value and a third probability for the third Q. And all the three probabilities will sum up to 1. And so we're going to do all this with sighed Max and sighed Max will attribute a large probability to the highest Q around. That's why an alternative to soft Max is a simple RMX not directly taking the maximum of the q values but in that case we're not exploring the other actions. Thanks to these probabilities we can explore somewhere else using a temperature parameter that we're going to see very quickly. We can still explore them by configuring this temperature parameter. That's why in general for security I highly recommend using a soft x rather than a simple RMX. All right so let's implement X and therefore as you understood. Since sought, Max returns the probabilities of each of the three Q values for the three possible actions. Well the first variable we are going to create is probably referring of course to these probabilities. So props equals and now we're going to take our sighed next function and according to you where are we going to take it from. Well of course remember we imported them. And then there is the functional submodule which I remember is the module that contains most of the actions to implement a neural network. We gave it the shortcut F and so that's actually from this functional submodule that we're going to take our self next function. But since we gave it a shortcut f we start here with a Neph representing the functional from which we take our sighed next function. Here it is. That's the first one and parenthesis. All right. Now what do we need to input in the next function? Well that's of course the entities for which we want to generate a probability distribution. And what are these entities? Well these are of course the key values. So now the question is how can we get the q values. Well of course the q values are the output of the neural network and to get these outputs of the neural network. Well here we go. We need to take our new network. But in fact we already have it because that's what initialized in the end it's function. Now we created a self-taught model which is nothing else that will not work because it is a new object of the network class. And so that's perfect. We can just take our model here and stuff next and apply this model to the input state which is the argument here and that will return the outputs that we're looking for. Those are the key values. And so now your intuition why we had to take the model here to introduce it in the function might get better. Those of you starting with object oriented programming you will see that all this will become natural so soft next then. So we take our models self because this must be the model of the object that we created here. But then we need to get the output of our neural network model and therefore we're going to hear some parenthesis in which we are going to input Well the input state named state here. So what we want to do at first is enter the state but now we must be careful that something looks like a simple set right now. But remember that state is actually going to be a torch sensor because later we're going to use this cell at less state to put it as the argument of the Select action function. The state's argument here is actually going to become later this self-taught state. And since this is a tortured answer world the model will accept it. So that's fine. But now we can improve the algorithm. So as soon as the state is a torch sensor and as we said earlier most of the sensors are wrapped into voivode. This will also contain a gradient. So right now what we're going to do first is wrap this input state that is a tensor into a torch very well but since this is the input state Well there is not going to be some differentiation. We will not be using the gradient of this state torch Voivode and that can be stations and therefore what we're going to do now is convert this torch sensor state into a torch variable like so. But then to specify that we don't want the gradients in the graph at all that can predict at the end of Mudgal. Well we will here come up volatile equals true. So now we have our state torched sensor into a torch very well but thanks to this Votel equals true barometer. Well we will be including the gradients associated to this input states to the graph of all the conditions of the end in that model. So that's another technical trick. This will save us some memory and therefore this will improve the performance. So I highly recommend doing this and now we're going to add something more fun. It's about this temperature parameter that I've just mentioned. So this temperature parameter is the parameter that would

268

allow us to modulate how the neural network will be sure of which action it should decide to play. So this temperature parameter will be a positive number and the closer it is to zero the less sure the neural network will be when playing in action and the higher the temperature parameter is the more sure the neural network will be of the action it decides to play. And to add this parameter I'm going to multiply the outputs which are the Kugan used by this temperature parameter. So let's start for example with 7 and I'm going to specify here the little comment T equals 7. So that's the temperature parameter. I'm sorry to go to 7. We're going to try some other ones but I just want to start with a small one because you're going to see that with a small one. Our car will still behave like some kind of an insect but then by increasing the temperature parameter our code will look more like a car and decides to sell driving will be much much better. And so that makes sense because the higher is this temperature parameter the higher will be the probability of the winning Juval me because for example if we have soft max of the q values. Let's take some simple numbers one two three if stuffed max of one to three equals. For example 0.04 0.11 and open eighty five. Then by increasing the temperature by taking higher temperatures. Right now temperature equals one by taking a high temperature like for example Tussaud subtracts let's copy this and multiply it by for example two or three so next have the same values but multiplied by the temperature parameter of three. Well we will get something like zero for the first Q value because this had a very low probability of something around zero then something very small for the second probability because this was still a low probability. So let's say for example or point 0 2. But then this third probability since it was the largest one and a pretty high one. Well increasing the temperature this probability will be even larger because we're going to be even more sure that this is the right Q value corresponding to the action we must play and therefore this is going to be something like 0.2 98. Now by increasing the temperature parameter Well we are now even more sure that the third action here should be the action to play because the probability for the q value of this action is not only the largest one but also very high. So that's what this temperature parameter is all about. It's about the certainty of which direction we should decide to play. All right. So I'm going to remove this comment. This was just to explain. And now let's get our act together. So how are you going to do that? Well the principle of the next method is not only to generate a probability distribution for each of the key values but also and that's the second step of the soft next method. We take a random draw from this distribution to get our final action. And of course we will have a high chance to get the action that corresponds to the Q value that has the highest probability because that's exactly how the distribution works. So there we go. Let's get our act together. So we're going to introduce a new Voivode that we're going to call action and this action is going to be a random draw of the probability distribution that we just created at this time before. And so how do we get such a random draw? Well we're going to take our prop's probabilities of each of the key values we take props and then dart and then we're going to use the multi Gnomeo function and that will give us a random draw from this distribution process. So that's all that will get his reaction. Perfect. And now of course we are going to return the action. There is a little trick here. What is the fact that this Propst that multinomial returns the PI towards viable with a fake badge. You know these fake diamonds are corresponding to the batch and therefore to get the right result that we want, that is the action in 0 1 or 2. We just need to add here data and then some brackets and the actions here are one or two that we're looking for is content and the index is 0 and 0. All right. And there we go. Now we have our action thanks to this select action function the AI will now know which action to play. And each time. Terrific. So now we can move on to the next function which will be the learn function. And that's where we will train the whole neural network you know with all the forward propagation and then the back propagation is to categorize in the sense. Well basically we will implement the whole training of the deep learning model that is at the heart of our artificial intelligence. So I can't wait to do that. This is going to be an exciting project and so I'll see you in the next Statoil.

SELF DRIVING CAR - STEP 11

Now in the next function that we're about implementing We will train the deep neural network that is inside our artificial intelligence. So basically we're going to do the whole process for propagation and then back propagation. So we're going to get our output. We're going to get the target. We'll compare the output of the target to compute the last error then we're going to back propagate this last error into the new network. And using suggested gradient descent who will have to wait according to how much they contributed to the last error. So let's do all this for those of you coming from the deep Marine Corps. This will be good stuff but for the others don't worry I'm going to expand that again. So we're going to call this new function learn and learn function is going to take several arguments. First self of course which will refer to the object of the degree in class. Then we're going to take our batched state for the current state then our batch next state then our That reward and finally Arbat action. So why do we take this? You probably recognized what this series is. Well that's of course a transition, a transition of the market decision process that is at the base. Did you learn? And why do we all take them into some batches? Well that's because you know remember we don't consider the transitions by a series of the top or current state next state current reward and current action. We created some simple batches here thanks to the simple function. And so now our transitions are in the form of the first batch for this state. A second batch for the next date, a batch for the reward and a batch for the action. That's the form of our transition's now and they're all well aligned with respect to time thanks to this concatenation that we made here with respect to the first dimension. So the point is now we have this transition of batches, one batch for each of the states. Next day we watch it in action and we do all this because we're using this experience replay trick. So that our deep neural network can learn something. Remember if you only had a transition by themselves what it would be some instant learning. Or if you want some very short memory learning and therefore the mole wouldn't learn anything. So we have to take these batches from the memory which become our transitions and then eventually we will get the different outputs for each of the states of the input states and we will do this for the states and for the next States because we will need both to compute the loss. I will soon remember the balance equation that is at the heart of the learning algorithm. So now let's go into the function and let's first get the outputs of the box state. So I'm going to call this first viable output and then we're going to say of course our self-talk is not all so self-start. No, because we want to get our model outputs of the input states of the state. And since our model is actually expecting a batch of input states. Well we can totally input that state right now for the input of them all. That's exactly how we initialized the states that are going into the network with torture answer with this vague dimension for the batch that's perfect. We now get the outputs of them all. But then there is another technical trick: if we only sell that model state well, we will get the outputs of all the possible actions you know 0 1 and 2 but that's not what we want. We are only interested in the actions that were chosen. The actions that were decided by the network to play at each time and so to get these actually interested in that is the actions played well we have to use this gather function in which we input one because we only want the action that was chosen and then we add that action with this one. And in that section we will gather each time the best action to play for each of the input states of the state. We don't want the action that is played, the action that is chosen and we get this with this gathering. But then be careful. The state here has this fake diamonds and grease on into the batch and that section doesn't have it. Backstay has it because we used to Unsworth with here but we haven't used any arm squeeze for the actions so we have to add it here so that the Bache action has the exact same dimension as the state. So we're going to add a dot and squeeze your right here and actually this is not zero but one because zero response to Faith is not the state and one will correspond to the examination of the actions. And finally the last thing we need to do here is we need to kill this fake batch with a squeeze. Why do we need to do that? Because now we are out of the neural network. We have our outputs but we don't want them back. We want them. And the simple answer is a simple vector. A vector of output the batches just when we work in the neural network because the neural network is expecting the format of sensors into a batch. But now we have our outputs and in the next Balun's equation of deep learning we won't need them in a batch. So I'm killing that here and killing the faith dimension to get back the simple form of our outputs. So I'm just adding here Dot and then squeeze and then since I want to kill the fake lamination corresponding to the back of the action. Well since the spacetime engine has index one I'm adding one here. All right. And now there we go we have our outputs. OK. We have a little warning that local variable output is assigned but never used. That's OK. We will use it very quickly. So that's our output. And now we want to get our next outwits So now you might be thinking why do we need the next outputs. Well to understand this we need to go back to the deep learning algorithm which is right here that is part of the letak handbook. So that's the whole diffusion process.

```python
32
33  class ReplayMemory(object):
34
35      def __init__(self, capacity):
36          self.capacity = capacity
37          self.memory = []
38
39      def push(self, event):
40          self.memory.append(event)
41          if len(self.memory) > self.capacity:
42              del self.memory[0]
43
44      def sample(self, batch_size):
45          samples = zip(*random.sample(self.memory, batch_size))
46          return map(lambda x: Variable(torch.cat(x, 0)), samples)
47
48  # Implementing Deep Q Learning
49
50  class Dqn():
51
52      def __init__(self, input_size, nb_action, gamma):
53          self.gamma = gamma
54          self.reward_window = []
55          self.model = Network(input_size, nb_action)
56          self.memory = ReplayMemory(100000)
57          self.optimizer = optim.Adam(self.model.parameters(), lr = 0.001)
58          self.last_state = torch.Tensor(input_size).unsqueeze(0)
59          self.last_action = 0
60          self.last_reward = 0
61
62      def select_action(self, state):
63          probs = F.softmax(self.model(Variable(state, volatile = True))*7) # T=7
64          action = probs.multinomial()
65          return action.data[0,0]
66
67      def learn(self, batch_state, batch_next_state, batch_reward, batch_action):
68          outputs = self.model(batch_state).gather(1, batch_action.unsqueeze(1)).squeeze(1)
69          |
70
71
```

At the beginning we were initializing all the key values and then at each time t. Well there we go we select the action with sighed Max that's what we did with the select action function. Then we opened the transition and then as you can see we got the prediction we got the target and we can be the last. So why do we need the next output as well? That's because of the target the target is equal to Ghana times the next output plus the we want and we will compute the targets right after that since we need the next output of the target. Let's compute this first. So again to get the next update very simple the next output is going to be the result of our neural network when the batched next state is entering it as input. So very simply we take our model that is our neural network and then this time the input of the neural network is going to be the batched next state that batches the next date. But now remember if we go back to the early algorithm Well you can see that the next output is the maximum of the q values for the next state with respect to all the actions. So right now to get the next output we need to get the maximum of these q values and therefore I'm going to do it here. Detach you know to detach all the outputs of the model because we have several states in this batch next States that's the batch of all the next states in all the transitions taken from the random sample of our memory. So I'm detaching all of them using the detach function and then I'm taking the max of all these two values. And since we're taking the maximum of these two values with respect to the action Well we have to specify that it is with respect to the action. And since the action is represented by the index one. Well again we have to put the next one here and then we have to specify that we're taking the cue values as T plus 1 that is the next stage and the next state is represented by 0 because the index zero corresponds to the states and therefore here we need to add brackets with index 0. That way we get the maximum of the key values of the next states represented by the next zero according to all the actions that are represented by the index one and now perfect we get our next outputs. These are a new set. That's when we had the warning. But that's fine. We will use it right now to compute the target. And speaking of the target, that's the next step of this known function. So there we go. Target equals. Now let's get back to our AI AI handbook. The target is equal to the word plus gamma times the next output is the maximum of the cube values of the next day. According to the actions that we can compute that. So that is equal to self that gamma and self that Gamma was initialized. Here it is introduced as a variable the Virgin Q. An object self gets to Times the next outputs as we just said plus Do we want that is the best want. We're working with batches here so plus the batch we want and that's the target. In one sample of the memory gamma multiplied by the next outputs Plus the reward. All right. Perfect. So now we have our outputs. We also have our targets and therefore we can compute the loss that is representing the error of the prediction. So let's call this last the last two is of course for the temporal difference. That is again at the heart of Q learning and this tiddy us is going to be equal to the release that improves the Cunanan. That's the last function we will choose for our artificial intelligence. For those of you coming from the deep green course that's really the last I recommend. If you want to implement the Coonerty and so how are we going to get this. Well again we're going to take a function from the functional module represented by F and therefore here I'm going to use our functional module f ducks and the Hubble us can be obtained thanks to the function Smoots L-1 loves that one. So pressing enter. And that's really the best lost function I recommend for deep learning. It really improves the Culin. But this is a function so I'm adding some parenthesis. And now there is nothing more simple. The arguments we need to input are the predictions and the targets. So the predictions of course are outputs because that's the output of the neural network. No, the output of the neural network is what the neural network predicts. So that's the prediction. So the first argument here is output and then the second argument is of course the target. The thing we're trying to get and it's already computed perfectly. We can directly input targets. Perfect. Now we have just told ourselves we've got a little tea here. There we go. Now the warning should disappear. Yes. Perfect. And now that we have the last error we can back propagators error back into the network to update the weights with stochastic gradient descent and that's exactly what we're going to do in the next step. So of course now what we have to do as you might guess is take our optimizing our optimizer which again we introduce you initialized it. And that's an atom optimizer which is actually an object of the Atom class and it is already fitted with the parameters of our model. And we already chose a learning rate of 0.1 percent to perfect our optimizer, but now we need to play it on the last error to perform a stochastic grid in the sense and data weights. So when working with fighters the first thing we need to do is re-initialize it at each iteration of the loop. We must reinitialize the optimizer from one interaction to the other in the loop of this to get the grid in the set and to re-initialize it. And each iteration of the loop. Well we're going to use the following method which is zero. Here we go. Zero grad will re-initialize the optimizer at each iteration of the loop. Then let's not forget the parenthesis. Perfect. And now that it is re-initialize Well we can perform backward propagation with our optimizer. And how do we do that? Well we take our laws and we're going to back propagate it back into the network and to back propagate into the network. We need to use the backward function and inside this backward function I recommend to input retain underscore variables and set it equal to true. I recommend doing this because this will improve back propagation. The use of written variables is true to free some memory and we need to free the memory because we are going to go several times on the last so that will definitely improve the training performance.

```python
30
31 # Implementing Experience Replay
32
33 class ReplayMemory(object):
34
35     def __init__(self, capacity):
36         self.capacity = capacity
37         self.memory = []
38
39     def push(self, event):
40         self.memory.append(event)
41         if len(self.memory) > self.capacity:
42             del self.memory[0]
43
44     def sample(self, batch_size):
45         samples = zip(*random.sample(self.memory, batch_size))
46         return map(lambda x: Variable(torch.cat(x, 0)), samples)
47
48 # Implementing Deep Q Learning
49
50 class Dqn():
51
52     def __init__(self, input_size, nb_action, gamma):
53         self.gamma = gamma
54         self.reward_window = []
55         self.model = Network(input_size, nb_action)
56         self.memory = ReplayMemory(100000)
57         self.optimizer = optim.Adam(self.model.parameters(), lr = 0.001)
58         self.last_state = torch.Tensor(input_size).unsqueeze(0)
59         self.last_action = 0
60         self.last_reward = 0
61
62     def select_action(self, state):
63         probs = F.softmax(self.model(Variable(state, volatile = True))*7) # 7=T
64         action = probs.multinomial()
65         return action.data[0,0]
66
67     def learn(self, batch_state, batch_next_state, batch_reward, batch_action):
68         outputs = self.model(batch_state).gather(1, batch_action.unsqueeze(1)).squeeze(1)
69         next_outputs = self.model(batch_next_state).detach().max(1)[0]
70         target = self.gamma*next_outputs + batch_reward
71         td_loss = F.smooth_l1_loss(outputs, target)
72         self.optimizer.zero_grad()
73         td_loss.backward(retain_variables = True)
74         self.optimizer.step()
75
76                         Arguments
77
78                         step(self, closure=None)
```

And finally the last step of this learned function is to have data weights according to the back propagation. That is according to how much the weights contributed to the error. And to do this we take our optimizer again which was initialized in re-initialize and we use the step function and simply with this line of code by using the step function. This will update the weights. That's this line of code that updates the weights. This line of code propagates the error into the neural network and this line of code uses the optimizer to update the weights and there we go. We have a learning neural network all right so congratulations. This was probably the most technical and difficult part of all this dispute or morrow. I know my torch can be tricky sometimes with ease and squeeze and squeeze but in the end I promise you will get a very functional neural network and therefore peculiarly model and eventually a great artificial intelligence. So now let's move on to the next step or teacher and model which will be the update function that will obviously update when the AI will discover the new state. So you know it will discover the new state and then it will receive the reward. Depending on the action that is displayed, this new state will take care of this with the update function and will do this in the next project.

SELF DRIVING CAR - STEP 12

All right so today we will be making the update function which will update everything there is to date as soon as the eye reaches a new state. So when it reaches a new stage you know we need to update the action. The last actually comes from the new action that was just played. But also the last date that becomes the new state. And finally the last word that becomes the new word we get when we play the action. So that's the logical path that happens right after selecting an action. We need to update all the elements of the transitions. And of course you'll get a new transition. So we will have to append this new transition to the memory. And finally we will also update our reward window to keep an eye on the evolution of how the training is going and how the exploration is going. But what's most important for you to understand is that now we can finally make a connection between the AI that we're implementing right now to our map because if we go back to our map remember there is this Beiji update function into the game class and that's where we were actually making the game with the car and defining how the car should be punished when it's making a mistake. But in this game class we noticed this update function and in this update function we noticed this line action because brain update last we worked less signal. And actually this is exactly what we're about to make. We are about to make this update function that will take the last word and the last signal to get the next action to play. So not only will they update all the different elements of the transition. But mostly we will be playing the action that we should play when getting the last word and the last signal and so of course in this update function we will use the select action function that we just implemented before we will integrate the select action function in the future update function that we're about to make to select direction to play besides making all the updates. So that's really important to make this connection with the map right now. What we're about to make is eventually the connection between our eyes and the game that we make in this class. And so what we can do now is directly take this update. Last we were less signal because that is actually the function that we'll be making with these two arguments here.

```python
93 class Ball2(Widget):
94     pass
95 class Ball3(Widget):
96     pass
97
98 # Creating the game class
99
100 class Game(Widget):
101
102     car = ObjectProperty(None)
103     ball1 = ObjectProperty(None)
104     ball2 = ObjectProperty(None)
105     ball3 = ObjectProperty(None)
106
107     def serve_car(self):
108         self.car.center = self.center
109         self.car.velocity = Vector(6, 0)
110
111     def update(self, dt):
112
113         global brain
114         global last_reward
115         global scores
116         global last_distance
117         global goal_x
118         global goal_y
119         global longueur
120         global largeur
121
122         longueur = self.width
123         largeur = self.height
124         if first_update:
125             init()
126
127         xx = goal_x - self.car.x
128         yy = goal_y - self.car.y
129         orientation = Vector(*self.car.velocity).angle((xx,yy))/180.
130         last_signal = [self.car.signal1, self.car.signal2, self.car.signal3, orientation, -orientatio
131         action = brain.update(last_reward, last_signal)
132         scores.append(brain.score())
133         rotation = action2rotation[action]
134         self.car.move(rotation)
135         distance = np.sqrt((self.car.x - goal_x)**2 + (self.car.y - goal_y)**2)
136         self.ball1.pos = self.car.sensor1
137         self.ball2.pos = self.car.sensor2
138         self.ball3.pos = self.car.sensor3
139
140         if sand[int(self.car.x),int(self.car.y)] > 0:
141             self.car.velocity = Vector(1, 0).rotate(self.car.angle)
142             last_reward = -1
143         else: # otherwise
```

287

And just as a quick reminder, the brain is our AI object, that is, it's the object of the Dejuan class. So what we're going to do now is we're going to copy this update less word less signal and that's going to be our next function we're making. And therefore and pasting that here then just to be careful I would just like to give some different names than the names we have here. You know we have the last word here and I don't want to confuse this last word with this one. That can be dangerous. So I'm going to replace last word here by word. And by the way, for less signal, let's just put a signal or even a new signal to specify that you know we want to measure that when reaching a new state and therefore getting a new signal. But then of course this word here is going to be the last reward that we get here. You know when going onto some sand or worse getting too close to one edge of the map that's where we define the last word. This last word is going to be the input of the update function so that's why we have the last word here. But right here I'm just giving another name for the argument. We want to not confuse it with the last word here. All right so this is the update function. And now let's go inside it and let's do these two things. That is to data all the elements of our transition and of course select the action. OK so what do we need to update first. Well as you understood we want to make a date when reaching any state. So the first thing we'll be updating is obviously this news that is the news that we were reaching. So I'm going to call this new state a new state and then it will. And so how can we get to this new state? Well of course that depends on the new signal that the sensors just detected. And as a reminder the state is the signal itself composed of the three signals that the sensors signal one signal to signal three plus orientation and minus orientation. That's our state. So be sure to understand that the signal is the state. But right now it is a simple list of five elements. And since this is going to be the input to do all that work remember we have to convert it into a torch sensor. So that's exactly what we're going to do right now. We are going to take our torch library and then take the tensor class there we go which will convert our new signal into a torch denser than it's better to make sure that all the elements of the torch to answer are floats so I'm going to make a type conversion to convert them into floats like this. And then finally try to get a reflex of what we need to do next. It's of course to create that fake down engine to add diamonds and correspond to the batch and we do this of course with the squeeze function to which we have to put the index of this big diamond. And we want a zero for the batch. All right. And now we have our new states composed of the three signals of the three sensors plus orientation minus orientation and of course that will depend on the new signal we are getting with this update function. Right at this time last signal we get the three signals. So in addition minus or in addition and as a reminder the three signals are the density of sensors detected around the sensors. All right. So we just got a new stage so that means we reached the new stage and now we have to make the next update. So according to you, what do we need to update now? What would be the logical thing to do right now after reaching this new state? Well what we need to date now is the memory. Why is that? It's because at each time t a transition is composed of the current state Estey the next day as tipis when the reward arti and the action 80. And right now we already have S-T we already have our team and we already have 80 and we just got the last element of the transition Estep plus one. So by getting this new state as deep as one we are getting one brand new transition of the memory and therefore we have to append this brand new transition to the memory because that's simply our next transition. So that's why we have that memory right now. And therefore what I'm going to do is take my memory object created from the replay memory class and therefore I'm going to take self memory to refer to the object. But since I'm using self I have to include the self in the of that function. So now you can really see what this self is for. It's whenever you use one variable that you created and initialized in the init function a that memory. And now we did it. And according to you how we're going to update that. Well the good news is that we already made a function to do that. It's the push function which bans an event or a transition to the memory. So that's exactly what we're going to use now. We're going to use the push function to open our new transition that we just made to the memory and therefore here I'm taking not an equal because we're going to use the method and therefore we can directly use that push. And first I'm going to add the transition to this new transition that we just got and that is first the last date. So self that last date. So that's S-T That's exactly this one it already exists. Then the next element of this transition is of course the new state that we just reached. And therefore since it is not viable of the object that we created and initialized in this init function we don't put itself here. We directly put the Newstead then the next element of the transition is the action and say we already have the last section which is this self that last action hero. So of course it is equal to zero. But then of course it will be updated with the select action function. But that's this one. So then it is self that last action. But now be careful. The elements that were included in this transition should all be torched answers. As you can see that's the case for the last date. It's a torch sensor. The new state is also torched answer. And so this must be the same for the action and then the reward of course. But now you're going to think how can it be a torched answer considering that it's simply a number. You know the action is either 0 1 or 2. But in fact that's not a problem. We can still convert this 0 1 or 2 variable into a torch sensor. This will just be what we call a long tensor. The long is a type and that's the tensor that will contain an integer because the last action is an integer it is 0 1 or 2. So what we're going to take now is our library torche then we're going to take the long is long tensor class that will create an object which will be the non-tenure itself. And by taking this self last action function as input it will create this long tensor object but it will still contain 0 1 or 2 into a long tensor object and that is just to be consistent with the transition that it only contains tensors because we're working with PI torch and we're working with a neural network. So we have to work with sensors so that we go torche long to answer. And one last conversion to make. We must be sure that what's inside this long answer is an integer and to make sure of it even if we already know that the last action is 0 1 or 2 to make sure that we are going to make this int type conversion again we convert our self last action into an integer. There we go and then we must just put that integer selfless action into brackets right here so that now we get a long tensor of one element which will be this last action 0 or 1 or 2 itself. So the key point is that's just how you convert a simple number zero one or two into a tensor with torche. All right. And then finally the last element of the transition and that's of course the last word we got. That's exactly the last word volleyball we created in any function that was initialized to zero. But then of course it is updated right here in this code either when we go on to some sense of a negative word or if we get further away from the goal that's again a negative reward. If we get closer to the goal that's a positive reward and the worst punishment if we get too close to one edge of the map. Well that's a terrible negative word minus one. And that's a.

```
46        return map(lambda x: Variable(torch.cat(x, 0)), samples)
47
48 # Implementing Deep Q Learning
49
50 class Dqn():
51
52     def __init__(self, input_size, nb_action, gamma):
53         self.gamma = gamma
54         self.reward_window = []
55         self.model = Network(input_size, nb_action)
56         self.memory = ReplayMemory(100000)
57         self.optimizer = optim.Adam(self.model.parameters(), lr = 0.001)
58         self.last_state = torch.Tensor(input_size).unsqueeze(0)
59         self.last_action = 0
60         self.last_reward = 0
61
62     def select_action(self, state):
63         probs = F.softmax(self.model(Variable(state, volatile = True))*7) # T=7
64         action = probs.multinomial()
65         return action.data[0,0]
66
67     def learn(self, batch_state, batch_next_state, batch_reward, batch_action):
68         outputs = self.model(batch_state).gather(1, batch_action.unsqueeze(1)).squeeze(1)
69         next_outputs = self.model(batch_next_state).detach().max(1)[0]
70         target = self.gamma*next_outputs + batch_reward
71         td_loss = F.smooth_l1_loss(outputs, target)
72         self.optimizer.zero_grad()
73         td_loss.backward(retain_variables = True)
74         self.optimizer.step()
75
76     def update(self, reward, new_signal):
77         new_state = torch.Tensor(new_signal).float().unsqueeze(0)
78         self.memory.push((self.last_state, new_state, torch.LongTensor([int(self.last_action)]), ))
79
80
```

So let's add this last element of the transition: self-direct the word. So I'm copying this pasting here and now we have to make another conversion which will be of course exactly the same as this one only since the word is not an integer but a float number. We will simply make a torch that tensor conversion but without that it will keep the brackets here because you know first we have to put the number into a list and then this list will go and put the torch into to class but we don't have to make that in conversion because last word is a float number. So what we're going to do is simply add here torche dot tensor torched a tensor then parenthesis brackets. And we are going to close the brackets here and we close the parenthesis. There we go. So to summarize Which did you say that we just reached and the we word we observe a new event of transition that we add to the memory. And this transition contains the last date and sees the new state as tipis when the last action plays 80 and the last word Archie. All right. And now we are going with our memory of dates.

SELF DRIVING CAR - STEP 13

All right so we just updated the memory after reaching the new state. And now let's take care of the next day. According to you now what is going to be the next update. Well basically we're done with one transition we have dated the last element of the transition which is the new state. So now it's like we're starting all over again. And when we were starting all over again. It's like you know we are in this new state of the environment and so what do we need to do now naturally. Well of course it's to play an action because we already got the observation of the news States. Now the thing that we have to do is play an action and therefore what we need to do now is of course use the select action function to play the action. So let's do it, let's create a new Voivode action and let's play the action with the select action I'm taking. Well first self to specify that the select action function is a method of the object of the class that will be created. So a self that selects action. Here we go. So that's the next action. And then of course since the select action function takes the state as input because of course the select action function will return the output of the neural network when the current input state enters the neural network.

So we have to input the input stage here and since that's the states that we just reached in the environment right now where the input state is of course you state because this state that we just reached at the time we right now is Newstead. So in this select action function I mean putting new sticks. All right so with this line of code we simply play the new action after reaching the new state. OK and now that we played an action Well we get the reward and therefore we get feedback with the reward. And therefore if we have more than 100 elements in the memory Well it would be time to learn. And therefore what we must do now is what logically comes after selecting an action which is of course to lower the AI needs to start learning. If it is doing things the right way. And now since it just played the action well we're going to make the AI learn from its actions in the last 100 events. But before we apply this learned function we have to make this condition to make sure that we already have reached more than 100 events because you know we're learning from the random samples of the memory. You know we have this huge memory of 10000 elements. We're taking some random samples of the memory of 100 elements and the AI is learning from the information contained in this sample of 100 random transitions. So let's just make this if condition to make sure that the number of elements of the memory of that memory and then be careful just a little trick here: self-taught memory is the object of your replay memory class but then the replay memory class has an attribute which is memory. So in fact we need to take some of the memory . The first memory is the object of the replay memory class and the second memory is the attribute here itself. So if the number of elements in the memory is well we want it to be larger than 100 then Cullin And then what happens. Well we can learn but for learning we need to get this random sample of 100 transitions and this we can get with the simple function. And since the simple function returns the different batches to states at time t this data 20 plus one the actions of time t and we were at 20. Well what we need to do now is create some new revivals which are going to be the batch of the states at time t the batch of the next dates the batch of the words and the batch of the actions and we can simply give the same names as we gave for the arguments here and they are here. And these variables will be equal to what the simple function returns because it returns exactly these batches and the state's next takes words and actions.

```
45          samples = zip(*random.sample(self.memory, batch_size))
46          return map(lambda x: Variable(torch.cat(x, 0)), samples)
47
48 # Implementing Deep Q Learning
49
50 class Dqn():
51
52      def __init__(self, input_size, nb_action, gamma):
53          self.gamma = gamma
54          self.reward_window = []
55          self.model = Network(input_size, nb_action)
56          self.memory = ReplayMemory(100000)
57          self.optimizer = optim.Adam(self.model.parameters(), lr = 0.001)
58          self.last_state = torch.Tensor(input_size).unsqueeze(0)
59          self.last_action = 0
60          self.last_reward = 0
61
62      def select_action(self, state):
63          probs = F.softmax(self.model(Variable(state, volatile = True))*7) # T=7
64          action = probs.multinomial()
65          return action.data[0,0]
66
67      def learn(self, batch_state, batch_next_state, batch_reward, batch_action):
68          outputs = self.model(batch_state).gather(1, batch_action.unsqueeze(1)).squeeze(1)
69          next_outputs = self.model(batch_next_state).detach().max(1)[0]
70          target = self.gamma*next_outputs + batch_reward
71          td_loss = F.smooth_l1_loss(outputs, target)
72          self.optimizer.zero_grad()
73          td_loss.backward(retain_variables = True)
74          self.optimizer.step()
75
76      def update(self, reward, new_signal):
77          new_state = torch.Tensor(new_signal).float().unsqueeze(0)
78          self.memory.push((self.last_state, new_state, torch.LongTensor([int(self.last_action)]), torc
79          action = self.select_action(new_state)
80          if len(self.memory.memory) > 100:
81              batch_state, batch_next_state, batch_reward, batch_action = self.memory.sample(100)
82              self.learn(batch_state, batch_next_state, batch_reward, batch_action)
83          self.last_action = action
84          self.last_state = new_state
85          self.last_reward = reward
86          self.reward_window.append(reward)
87          if len(self.reward_window) > 1000:
88              del self.reward_window[0]
89          return action
90
```

So what we simply need to do now is get first our memory object and then from this memory object we are going to use the simple method which will take as inputs. Well the number of transitions we want our AI to learn from that is 100. That's why we made sure that we had more than one hundred transitions. So it's going to learn from 100 transitions of the memory. So the learning will be much better. And so now let's make this really happen. Well since the learn method is a method of our in class.

Well we need to access this Learn method from the future objects that will be created from a different class and therefore what we need to take is self. Self refers to that objective to do during class and then learn as this learned method learned method to which when out Of course these guys here the bad state the Belgian state the natural world and the Bachche action. These are our batches sampled from our memory and we get 100 of them because we have 100 transitions from these 100 transitions we take 100 States 100 next states 100 reward and 100 actions let's face the here and there we go now the learning will happen. It will happen from all these random batches. Perfect. And now what we need to do is the very last updates after you know reaching a new state and playing in action. Well we got you actually to play but we still didn't have that reaction. That is our self that last action voivode. So let's make sure we don't forget this. Let's do it right now. We will update the last action self that last action equals and of course the action that we just stay here with this select action function. All right now the last section is updated. Same for the new state. We reached the new state but we haven't updated the last date yet because of course the last was before the state at time t. But now we have reached the new state surplus when it's time to pass one. Well the last it becomes this you said here. Therefore we need to update as well. Self that last state equals our new state. There we go. And now what do we need to date? Well there is only one thing left. That's of course the word and the word is exactly the word we get in reality. So that will be the argument of this function which if we made the connection to our map will be the last word. That is the word we get right after playing the action in this new state. So if we go on to some sound this last word will be that minus one if we get further from the go we will get a slightly bad word minus 0.2 if we get closer to the goal. We will get a slightly good reward 0.1. And if we get too close to an edge of the map, well that will be about punishment. We will get minus one for each. So that's the last word we get. In reality that is when that happens for real on the map. And this will be the argument of the function. The last word here. That's exactly this one. And since this is the argument of the update function that corresponds to this we weren't here and therefore our self that last word variable initialized at the beginning in this function becomes the new word we get in reality that is the word or that's the same last word. All right. Now we updated our last word. And now since we just got our last word. Well we can now date the world. You remember the war when we initialized here as one of the variables of the object of our class. That's the window that's going to keep track of how this train is going by taking the average of the last 100 rewards. So you know it will be like a sliding window showing us how the meaning of the world is evolving. And so since we just got our last word. Well we can update the we were window into how do we update it. Well we simply need to append this last word to the window and therefore what I'm going to do is take my war window self that we word when they hear this and I'm going to use the append function. And inside the open function we need to input the element we want to append to the we were when doing that of course do we want. All right, perfect. And then since this war window is going to have a fixed size you know it's not going to be a growing window it's going to be a window of fixed size sliding with time to show the evolution of the world. And so now we need to decide on the size of this winter. And it's simply the number of means of the reward we will have in this window. And so for example let's get you know the last 1000 means of the last 100 words. And so to make sure of it we're going to add if then plan then we take our work window and we simply add here if the number of elements in the window is larger than 1000. Well what we want to do is delete the first element of this who our window and the first element of this where window has to index zero. All right. Now we make sure that this war window will never get more than 1000 elements. There is one thousand means of the last 100 words that's perfect. This will be a window of fixed size so that we can see if the mean of the word is increasing. And therefore if the training is going well and accordingly the court does what we want. Perfect. And now one tiny little thing left to do according to you is what it is going to be. Well remember this update function not only updates the different elements of the transition in the war window but also it returns the action that was played when reaching this new state. That's why we have and then that action equals bring that date that we're less signal and therefore it's supposed to return something and the something that is supposed to return is of course the action. So the simple last thing we need to do here is just return to the action that was just played when reaching the new stage. And that's when our update function is ready. It's going to do all the required updates and it will turn the action when reaching the new stage. That's perfect. That was the last difficult action to make for all this a process. Now the rest will be good stuff. We will just make a core function to return the means that we want in the window. Then we will make a safe function to save the brain of the car whenever you want to quit the application and go back to it. And of course since you want to be able to load the brain of your car when you get back to it get back to the application. Well we will end up by making a load function which will load your model after you save your model with the same function. So three functions to do that but it's going to be simple. And then we'll have the most exciting section of this first module that is the demo we will see if the air works. We will see if the car reaches the goals and we will see how we can improve it and then eventually you will have to build your first AI. So I can't wait to start the demo.

SELF DRIVING CAR - STEP 14

All right, a very quick project today to make this core function. And so basically this function will just compute the score on the sliding window of the reward. And so basically we will very simply compute the mean of all the rewards in the reward window. So this will be very simple. Let's do this. Now we're going to make this new function that we're going to call core and this core function will just take the argument itself because basically we don't need anything. We need to take cells because of course we will take self-talk. We were winda so just self and then Cullin and there we went. It's going to take one line of code. So we want to compute the mean of all the words in the window. So that's basically the sum of all the words in this window that are between minus 1 plus 1 divided by the total number of elements in this window.

```python
48 # Implementing Deep Q Learning
49
50 class Dqn():
51
52     def __init__(self, input_size, nb_action, gamma):
53         self.gamma = gamma
54         self.reward_window = []
55         self.model = Network(input_size, nb_action)
56         self.memory = ReplayMemory(100000)
57         self.optimizer = optim.Adam(self.model.parameters(), lr = 0.001)
58         self.last_state = torch.Tensor(input_size).unsqueeze(0)
59         self.last_action = 0
60         self.last_reward = 0
61
62     def select_action(self, state):
63         probs = F.softmax(self.model(Variable(state, volatile = True))*7) # T=7
64         action = probs.multinomial()
65         return action.data[0,0]
66
67     def learn(self, batch_state, batch_next_state, batch_reward, batch_action):
68         outputs = self.model(batch_state).gather(1, batch_action.unsqueeze(1)).squeeze(1)
69         next_outputs = self.model(batch_next_state).detach().max(1)[0]
70         target = self.gamma*next_outputs + batch_reward
71         td_loss = F.smooth_l1_loss(outputs, target)
72         self.optimizer.zero_grad()
73         td_loss.backward(retain_variables = True)
74         self.optimizer.step()
75
76     def update(self, reward, new_signal):
77         new_state = torch.Tensor(new_signal).float().unsqueeze(0)
78         self.memory.push((self.last_state, new_state, torch.LongTensor([int(self.last_action)]), torch.
79         action = self.select_action(new_state)
80         if len(self.memory.memory) > 100:
81             batch_state, batch_next_state, batch_action, batch_reward = self.memory.sample(100)
82             self.learn(batch_state, batch_next_state, batch_reward, batch_action)
83         self.last_action = action
84         self.last_state = new_state
85         self.last_reward = reward
86         self.reward_window.append(reward)
87         if len(self.reward_window) > 1000:
88             del self.reward_window[0]
89         return action
90
91     def score(self):
92         return sum(self.reward_window)/(len(self.reward_window)+1.)
93
```

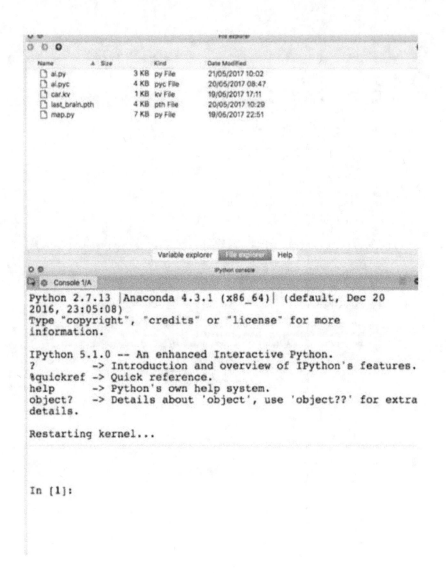

```
Name           ▲ Size      Kind        Date Modified
  ai.py          3 KB  py File     21/05/2017 10:02
  ai.pyc         4 KB  pyc File    20/05/2017 08:47
  car.kv         1 KB  kv File     19/06/2017 17:11
  last_brain.pth 4 KB  pth File    20/05/2017 10:29
  map.py         7 KB  py File     19/06/2017 22:51
```

Variable explorer   File explorer   Help

Python console

Console 1/A

```
Python 2.7.13 |Anaconda 4.3.1 (x86_64)| (default, Dec 20
2016, 23:05:08)
Type "copyright", "credits" or "license" for more
information.

IPython 5.1.0 -- An enhanced Interactive Python.
?          -> Introduction and overview of IPython's features.
%quickref -> Quick reference.
help       -> Python's own help system.
object?    -> Details about 'object', use 'object??' for extra
details.

Restarting kernel...


In [1]:
```

So let's do this. We are directly going to return that. So in starting with we turn and so we need to take the sum of all the words in the window and to do this we simply need to take the we were Windu itself and so on inputting herself that reward window. All right. And so very simply this will sum all the elements inside the window. That's pretty practical. And then to get the mean we need to divide this sum by the number of elements in the window and to get the number of elements. Well we need to take the len function and then we say are we were window again. There it is. But now we just need to be Yahoo with something that lends itself. The window is a denominator and this must absolutely not be equal to zero no matter what we need to avoid this and to make sure that the denominator here is not equal to zero. We are going to add this safety trick. We're going to add a plus one here so that Lancefield that we won't win window plus one will never be equal to zero if the denominator is equal to zero. This will crash your system. So we must avoid it and that's totally fine. Our plus one will still get a good measure of the score. All right, perfect. And so that's all we have. Our school function which will give us the meaning of the reward in the sliding window. All right. Now let's move on to the next function which is the same function that will save your model that is said to be the brain of your car so that you can then be able to reuse it by loading it with another function that will make after this a function. So it's really practical to have this safe function to save your miles in case you want to reuse them for any kind of purpose where they can be useful.

SELF DRIVING CAR - STEP 15

All right so today we're going to make a function that will save or model that is that will save the brain of the car so that we can we use it whenever we quit the application. Thanks to the Save function will be able to save the model. Then quit the application and then when we go back to the application things to another function that is the load function which will make after this one we will be loading the last version of our model that was trained so that will be very practical and therefore let's make these two functions the same function and the load function. So let's start with the same function in this project. So here comes the new def then save and then it's going to take one argument that it's going to be self. And the reason is that the thing we are going to say is not the whole model here but our neural network Selldorf model and our optimizer cells that optimize it because what we want to save is just the last weights that were dated at the last iteration because whenever we want to reuse our saved more later we wanted to bring the action to play with the weights that were already trained. So we need to take this last version of the weights. And also we need to take the last version of the optimizer because it is connected to these weights. So let's do this. We have our cells so we'll be able to take our That model in ourselves the optimizer and we will be saving these two objects in a Python dictionary and to save these two objects. We're going to use the same function from the torch module. So I'm starting here with torche that save and in parenthesis we are going to put that dictionary brackets in a dictionary. Bison works like that you have a key which is your identifier. So that's unique. And for each you have the value you want to get to that key. So it's like a mapping function from unique identifiers to a value you want to get these identifiers. If you take a simple dictionary book well the keys will be the words and the values will be the definitions of the words. Well here that's to say we're going to make two keys, one key for the first object we want to save which is the subduct model and one second before. The second thing we want to say is that we are optimizers and therefore let's start with the first key. So we had to give a name to that key and I'm going to call it state on the score dict because then you're going to see them going to use the function say dict to save our model in the dictionary. So that's our first key then to give the value we want to attribute for that first key. Well as you can see I added a little con here and here I'm going to add the object I want to say. So the first object I want to say is self model so we can just copy this self to morrow and paste it as the value of our first key cell. Now then we add that state underscore dict. Here we go. The first one. And then we add in parenthesis and that will save the parameters of your model. In this first key state dict. And now let's say our optimizer. So we're going to add a second key in the dictionary and to do this we have here a comma. Then press enter and then we go with our second key. So the second key We're going to call it. Well we can call it optimizer then call in and then we just need to add the name of the object you want to save. And that is self. That is our optimizer. So we add here self that optimizer. And then again to set the parameters of this optimizer we are here again in that state. And then we go we have our model saved with all the weight saved and our optimizer saves perfect and then we will save all this into a file and to do this I'm going to add a second argument to the Save function which is going to be the name of this file where we want to have our model in our optimizer set. So remember I should do a quick demo in the first section of this first module self-driving car. You know that was a demo where we just had some random actions. So that was not yet the self-driving car but then remember I clicked on the save button to save the model and this created the last brain that PCH found which is the file that contains the same version of your email.

```
48 # Implementing Deep Q Learning
49
50 class Dqn():
51
52     def __init__(self, input_size, nb_action, gamma):
53         self.gamma = gamma
54         self.reward_window = []
55         self.model = Network(input_size, nb_action)
56         self.memory = ReplayMemory(100000)
57         self.optimizer = optim.Adam(self.model.parameters(), lr = 0.001)
58         self.last_state = torch.Tensor(input_size).unsqueeze(0)
59         self.last_action = 0
60         self.last_reward = 0
61
62     def select_action(self, state):
63         probs = F.softmax(self.model(Variable(state, volatile = True))*7) # T=7
64         action = probs.multinomial()
65         return action.data[0,0]
66
67     def learn(self, batch_state, batch_next_state, batch_reward, batch_action):
68         outputs = self.model(batch_state).gather(1, batch_action.unsqueeze(1)).squeeze(1)
69         next_outputs = self.model(batch_next_state).detach().max(1)[0]
70         target = self.gamma*next_outputs + batch_reward
71         td_loss = F.smooth_l1_loss(outputs, target)
72         self.optimizer.zero_grad()
73         td_loss.backward(retain_variables = True)
74         self.optimizer.step()
75
76     def update(self, reward, new_signal):
77         new_state = torch.Tensor(new_signal).float().unsqueeze(0)
78         self.memory.push((self.last_state, new_state, torch.LongTensor([int(self.last_action)]), torch
79         action = self.select_action(new_state)
80         if len(self.memory.memory) > 100:
81             batch_state, batch_next_state, batch_action, batch_reward = self.memory.sample(100)
82             self.learn(batch_state, batch_next_state, batch_reward, batch_action)
83         self.last_action = action
84         self.last_state = new_state
85         self.last_reward = reward
86         self.reward_window.append(reward)
87         if len(self.reward_window) > 1000:
88             del self.reward_window[0]
89         return action
90
91     def score(self):
92         return sum(self.reward_window)/(len(self.reward_window)+1.)
93
94     def save(self):
95         torch.save({'state_dict': self.model.state_dict(),
96                     'optimizer': self.optimizer.state_dict,
97                    }, 'last_brain.pth')
```

311

```
Name            ▲ Size        Kind          Date Modified
☐ ai.py           3 KB  py File      21/05/2017 10:02
☐ ai.pyc          4 KB  pyc File     20/05/2017 08:47
☐ car.kv          1 KB  kv File      19/05/2017 17:11
☐ last_brain.pth  4 KB  pth File     20/05/2017 10:29
☐ map.py          7 KB  py File      19/05/2017 22:51
```

```
                    Variable explorer   File explorer   Help
                              Python console
  Console 1/A

Python 2.7.13 |Anaconda 4.3.1 (x86_64)| (default, Dec 20
2016, 23:05:08)
Type "copyright", "credits" or "license" for more
information.

IPython 5.1.0 -- An enhanced Interactive Python.
?           -> Introduction and overview of IPython's features.
%quickref -> Quick reference.
help        -> Python's own help system.
object?    -> Details about 'object', use 'object??' for extra
details.

Restarting kernel...




In [1]:
```

So I'm going to add here last underscore brain that age so
that your moral and your optimizer will be saved into this
created file. Let's bring that page so you don't have it yet.
But as soon as you said your model on the application this

file will be created thanks to this code we just added. All right. And so now perfect. We have a safe function that will save your model, save the brain of your car by saving the weights and the optimizer of the new network that is in fact the brain of the car so perfect we now have only one function to create left. That's the load function and that's because the same function never goes without a load function. No, there is no purpose in saving your model. If you cannot load what you say afterwards. So that's the last step in our journey before the exciting demo and we will make this Sloat function.

SELF DRIVING CAR - STEP 16

We're going to make the last function of this D2 in class which is going to be of course the load function that naturally comes after the same function. You save your model and then you want to be able to load it whenever you go back to the application. So let's do this. We're going to make def then load. We call the class function load again this load function will take as arguments self and you probably guess where this self will be for it will be exactly to load what was saved in the same function. So we will take self-direct tomorrow. And of course solve that optimizer. So the self-heal will be for the model and the optimizer. So then Cullin And now let's slow the model. So since Dymo is in the last brindled ph file we want to make sure this file exists and therefore that's what we're going to start with. We're going to make an IF condition to make sure that this file exists and if it exists we will be loading what we have in the dictionary which is in this last print PDA. So we start with an if then we're going to take our operating system and the path leading to this last brain that PVH found. So that path is exactly the path that leads to the working directory folder. So as far as I'm concerned, that's a faster desktop than my artificial intelligence. It is a folder then model one self-driving car and then the module one self-driving car folder. There is this folder here with the last print that you found. And then we're going to add to what is a file file this one. So that's a function. So I'm going to add some parenthesis. And inside the parenthesis I'm going to input the name of the file name of the file that contains the model that is the last brain death. So we have to put it in quotes. And so I'm entering the last brain that dies and so is the last brain. That page will return true if the file that's friend that age exists and falls if it doesn't exist and therefore this condition means if we have the last render. Well now working directory folder then let's go. What's going to happen in that case? In that case if this file exists. Well first we're going to print something to say that you know we're loading the morals of for example you can say a little arrow and then loading checkpoints with three little dots. All right. That's just to say we're loading tomorrow. And then of course we're going to load the model. So the moral and the optimizer and we're going to put what we load in a will that I'm going to call checkpoint equals and that's where we're going to use the load function to load what was saved in the same function. So of course this is a function from the torch library to torch dot and the name of the Sloat function is simply that parentheses and inside the parentheses according to you what we need to input. Well very simply we need to input the file that contains our saved tomorrow and are saved optimizing optimizer so we simply need to put the name of the file which is last bring dot de-th. Let's bring that BGH and we load this file only in the condition that this file exists. So that's why we had to call this condition here. OK so now that we loaded the model and the optimizer. Well what we're going to do is update separately our model and the optimizer because actually we loaded the parameters we loaded the weights and the parameters of the optimizer. So now what we need to do is update our existing model which is this one cell block model and our existing optimizer solved that optimizer with the parameters with the weights that are in this last Brender. So we simply need to make these two update separately and to do this we're going to use a method from the torture modules. So there's going to be inheritance which will allow us to use this method that is called Load state dict and the slowed static method will allow us to date all the parameters of our model and our optimizer. So let's do this and let's start by updating our models. So we take our model which is a self taught model since the self-taught model inherits from the methods of the torch module to use the load state dict method. So that's the method we're taking from the inheritance. And thanks to this method we are going to update all the parameters of the model that is all the way. And so what we need to put in this state Dick method is our checkpoint very well. That is the result of the load function. So checkpoints then brackets and now we need to enter the name of the key that corresponds to our model that corresponds to the subducted model state date. And that is the state. So in checkpoints and the brackets we enter in quote States underscore tickets and this line of code will update your model. That is a tool that awaits the parameters of your model. And now we need to do the same for the optimizer. And that's going to be almost the same. So I'm going to copy this line pasted below. And so this time we're going to date not tomorrow but the optimizer. Then again we use the state Dick method that inherits from the torch module methods and we apply this function to the checkpoint of the state dict. But the key that corresponds to the optimizer and that is the optimizer. So here we just replace a date by up to Mixer. There we go. Here we update the weights of the. And here we update the parameters of the optimizer. Perfect and then just to finish we can print a little done like that. And finally we just need to specify what happens if this condition is not respected. That is if there are not a lot of Pythia trials and so we just need to add an other than Colin and Cindy we're just going to say that there is no such file. Let's bring the PTA age. So we're just going to print something like No check point out and three little ones if you want.

```python
            next_outputs = self.model(batch_next_state).detach().max(1)[0]
            target = self.gamma*next_outputs + batch_reward
            td_loss = F.smooth_l1_loss(outputs, target)
            self.optimizer.zero_grad()
            td_loss.backward(retain_variables = True)
            self.optimizer.step()

    def update(self, reward, new_signal):
        new_state = torch.Tensor(new_signal).float().unsqueeze(0)
        self.memory.push((self.last_state, new_state, torch.LongTensor([int(self.last_action)]), torch
        action = self.select_action(new_state)
        if len(self.memory.memory) > 100:
            batch_state, batch_next_state, batch_action, batch_reward = self.memory.sample(100)
            self.learn(batch_state, batch_next_state, batch_reward, batch_action)
        self.last_action = action
        self.last_state = new_state
        self.last_reward = reward
        self.reward_window.append(reward)
        if len(self.reward_window) > 1000:
            del self.reward_window[0]
        return action

    def score(self):
        return sum(self.reward_window)/(len(self.reward_window)+1.)

    def save(self):
        torch.save({'state_dict': self.model.state_dict(),
                    'optimizer': self.optimizer.state_dict,
                   }, 'last_brain.pth')

    def load(self):
        if os.path.isfile('last_brain.pth'):
            print("=> loading checkpoint...")
            checkpoint = torch.load('last_brain.pth')
            self.model.load_state_dict(checkpoint['state_dict'])
            self.optimizer.load_state_dict(checkpoint['optimizer'])
            print("done !")
        else:
            print("no checkpoint found...")
```

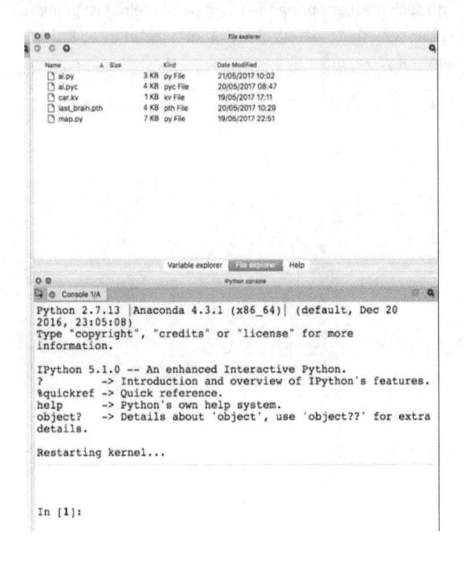

```
Name          ▲ Size        Kind          Date Modified
  ai.py         3 KB  py File    21/05/2017 10:02
  ai.pyc        4 KB  pyc File   20/05/2017 08:47
  car.kv        1 KB  kv File    19/05/2017 17:11
  last_brain.pth 4 KB pth File   20/05/2017 10:29
  map.py        7 KB  py File    19/06/2017 22:51
```

Variable explorer   File explorer   Help

Python console

Console 1/A

```
Python 2.7.13 |Anaconda 4.3.1 (x86_64)| (default, Dec 20
2016, 23:05:08)
Type "copyright", "credits" or "license" for more
information.

IPython 5.1.0 -- An enhanced Interactive Python.
?          -> Introduction and overview of IPython's features.
%quickref -> Quick reference.
help       -> Python's own help system.
object?    -> Details about 'object', use 'object??' for extra
details.

Restarting kernel...


In [1]:
```

All right. And that gives us a functional load function and mostly functional. Did you in class and now huge congratulations because our artificial intelligence is ready you can probably hear by the sound of my voice and I'm getting very excited because now it's time for the demo.

We just made a brain and we're going to put this brain in the car and we will see how it is clever enough to do these round trips between the airport and downtown wherever the road is. So I can't wait to show you the demo.

SELF DRIVING CAR - LEVEL 1

It's going to be epic. We're going to test our eye on the environment and we're going to test it on four different levels. That is we're going to play a game. The game will have four levels of difficulty and the aim will be to pass these four levels. So we're going to be these four levels. First Level One the first level is going to be to reach the airport and then do some round trips between the airport and the downtown. So as soon as we see the car do these round trips Well we pass level 1 then Level 2 Level 2 will be to still do these round trips. But on the specific road that we draw ourselves but it's going to be an easy road because it's level 2. And of course the car will have to self-drive by staying on that road. So it will be a road that goes from the airport to downtown and then the other way. And so the car will have to do these round trips by sitting on that road. If it does we will pass level 2 and level 3. Level 3 will be to draw some obstacles on the map to see if the car manages to avoid the obstacles and still reach its goal.

```python
1 # AI for Self Driving Car
2
3 # Importing the libraries
4
5 import numpy as np
6 import random
7 import os
8 import torch
9 import torch.nn as nn
10 import torch.nn.functional as F
11 import torch.optim as optim
12 import torch.autograd as autograd
13 from torch.autograd import Variable
14
15 # Creating the architecture of the Neural Network
16
17 class Network(nn.Module):
18
19     def __init__(self, input_size, nb_action):
20         super(Network, self).__init__()
21         self.input_size = input_size
22         self.nb_action = nb_action
23         self.fc1 = nn.Linear(input_size, 30)
24         self.fc2 = nn.Linear(30, nb_action)
25
26     def forward(self, state):
27         x = F.relu(self.fc1(state))
28         q_values = self.fc2(x)
29         return q_values
30
31 # Implementing Experience Replay
32
33 class ReplayMemory(object):
34
35     def __init__(self, capacity):
36         self.capacity = capacity
37         self.memory = []
38
39     def push(self, event):
40         self.memory.append(event)
41         if len(self.memory) > self.capacity:
42             del self.memory[0]
43
44     def sample(self, batch_size):
45         samples = zip(*random.sample(self.memory, batch_size))
46         return map(lambda x: Variable(torch.cat(x, 0)), samples)
47
48 # Implementing Deep Q Learning
49
```

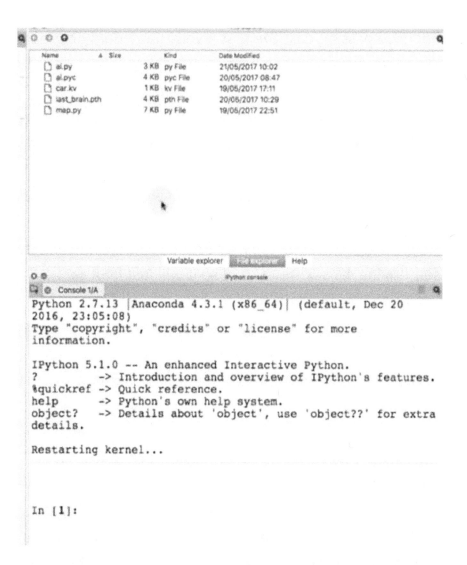

So no worries will draw some difficult obstacles that the car will have to avoid. And we'll see if it manages to reach the airport and the downtown and finally the most challenging level for the car will be to draw a very difficult road to reach the downtown. So I don't know if you know it will be a road like some zigzag. I'm not a brilliant architect but I'll try to make a challenging road. So let's hope we pass at least the first level. That would be great. Then let's hope we can also pass level two and three. And if we passed level 4 that would be wonderful. So let's do this, let's take the challenge. Well actually the self-driving car is going to take the challenge but we are the brains behind this. So let's tell how that works. All right so the first thing I'm going to do is just to give you a quick reminder about the map. So that's the map. And first we're going to look at the map we're going to look at the self-driving car without the AI so it will just be a car having those random actions that you saw at the beginning of this model. So how can we look at that? Well we have to deactivate the AI and the activity. We simply need to put a temperature equal to zero. Remember that the parameter here is the temperature. And right now it is equal to seven. That's a low temperature. We will increase that afterward. But if we don't want the car to have a brain, that is if we don't want to activate the AI we simply need to set the temperature to zero equals zero. And same here of course that's the real temperature in the cold too. There we go. And then we must not forget to say because otherwise that won't include the change. I guess now we don't have any. I see I used to activate it. So let's have a look at the map just to give us a quick refresher. A quick reminder about what it looks like. So I'm going to select everything and press enter. All right. And there's our map and there is our car. So as you can see the car is having totally random actions. You know to go left to go straight to the right and therefore it is not reaching the airport which is, as I remember, at the upper left of the map and not reaching it. Well it just did. That's totally random. You see it right now it is at the airport and it is not reaching the other goal which is downtown at the bottom right of the map. So we were just like here but we can clearly see now that the actions are totally random. It is going nowhere and there is definitely no artificial intelligence but no worries. We will activate it right now.

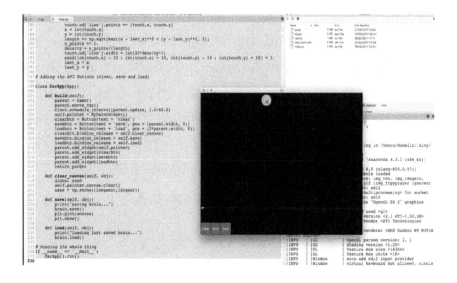

I'm going to close the map and then I'm going to restart the kernel and restart DeCarlo. You click on this tool button here and then yes. And now time for the show we're finally going to put this train we made in the car and activate the AI. I'm super excited to see what's going to happen. We're going to activate the air right now and to do this we need to raise the temperature so to change the temperature which is replaced at zero by well let's start with seven as we had before. So let's specify seven here. All right let's not forget to say. And now let's get back to our map and now we can just re-execute this again because we restarted the kernel. So let's say it. And there we go we have the car. And what is it doing? Well it is trying to find its way, it's exploring its understanding of what it has to do and it's about to reach the airport and there we first go. It's wonderful and now the next goal is to reach downtown and the dead just reach downtown. And now it's trying to find the airport back going to the airport and there again Wonderfalls that works. It didn't take time actually to explore and learn from the mistakes you know the mistake here is to get further from the go. That's where we punish the car by giving it a slightly negative reward. You know it's minus 0.2.

So it learned from that mistake and by learning from that mistake it managed to get the positive rewards by getting closer to the goal. And now it finally understands what it has to do. It's definitely reaching the airport and then reaching downtown and then doing these round trips. That's perfect. We have a self-driving car but I cannot help but notice it is looking like an insect. The car doesn't really seem sure of itself. No, it doesn't have a very confident movement. It's like your left and right that's not moving like a car movement. It looks more like a bug. So we're going to fix that. And as you might have guessed the way to fix that is to increase the temperature because remember the temperature is the parameter in the soft Mac function that we can increase so that the action is returned with more certainty. So that makes sense that if we increase temperature well we might end up getting a car more sure of itself because the AI will be more sure of which action it should play. And that remember is because the action will be played with a higher probability. The only problem with increasing the temperature is that remember the AI is less exploring the other actions because by increasing the temperature of the other actions we'll have low probabilities. But right now that doesn't seem to be a problem because the car seems to have no problem reaching its goals. The airport is downtown so we can totally increase the temperature if we want this thing that so far looks like an insect looks like a car. So let's do this. I'm going to close this now. There we go. Restart the kernel again. And press yes. And now we're going to increase the temperature. So let's do this. I'm going back to my file then replacing seven by 100 There we go. Then we save. And now we have a self-driving car sure of itself. So we might get better results and we might get something that looks more like a car. Let's take a map and then let's do that again. All right, what's happened? OK. It did some kind of a burnout. Not sure why. But anyway now we have something that looks more like a car. You can see that it is going more straight. It is not doing these quick left and right movements. That's because now the car is more sure of which direction to take and each time you know it wants to take the best direction going to the airport and then to downtown. So clearly we can now say that we passed level one. The car is doing these round trips between the airport and downtown. So we are going to save that. I'm going to show you how to save the brain. We just need to click on this save button and if we look at what happens here. Well we have the curve of the we were at the beginning we can observe some mistakes that it made. So that's where the reward is negative. But then it learned from its mistakes and the reward increased little by little until reaching a constant positive reward equals to open one but that's the maximum reward we set. And that's because it ended up exploring. That's the expiration phase. And then it just knew what it had to do. That's where it was doing these round Rountree between the airport and the downtown without any mistake. So there we go. We passed level one. Congratulations. Now let's get things more challenging. Let's take things at the next level. Let's try to pass the level to which I remind you we do these round trips on a specific road. We're going to draw ourselves.

SELF DRIVING CAR - LEVEL 2

Are you ready to take level 2? Are you excited? Well me too. Let's do this. As you can notice I just quit the application but that's not a problem because we saved the last brain so we're going to go back to the app and load the last brain and this will have the last weight of the neural networks like you know it will have the last Sinapis of the brain. So it will already know how to do the round trips between the airport and the downtown. But now we're taking on the challenge of passing level 2. So as a reminder Level two is to still do the round trips. But by staying on a specific road that we will draw ourselves right now in the Statoil. So let's see if it can do that. Let's make this road simple because then remember that Level 4 is a highly complicated road. So for now that will still be nice with our self-driving car. All right, let's do this. It's already selected and going to select that over again. And let's try to beat level 2. There we go. It's doing weird spinning for us but that's because I didn't know that. Let's load the brain and there we go. Now it should be OK. Yes it is. It's doing the round trips between the airport. There we go. And now to downtown. It's going downtown and perfect and now doing the other round trips. All right. So that's level one. And now let's take care of level two. So I'm going to draw a road something like this so let me think what to draw. It has to be simple. So what about something like this? I told you I'm not a very good architect. But I am trying to do something not too difficult. Something like that. What do you think? All right. So that's the other order of the road. Not something like this. And there we go. All right. Pretty good. Well that's a classic road but OK. So it's on the road. Perfect. And so now the challenge is not to cross some sand. So here we go. First mistake. But I'm going to learn from this mistake and try not to do it again. If we actually save the brain we can see the mistake probably. Yes. If we look at it well, we see the mistakes it made here. That's where it crossed some sand probably. So there we go. Right now it's on the road and it's reaching the goals. Right now it just reached downtown and is going back on the road to reach the airport. There we go. Perfect Job well done.

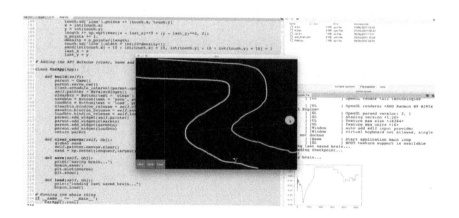

So it seems that level 2 has passed already. Didn't take much time to do the training. So that's great. That's great. We can take it to the next level now. Yes indeed. The round trips look perfect. We can still send some hesitations. Maybe we can still increase the temperature. But you know it's reaching the goals and staying on the road. It's not make any sense. So that's definitely a self-driving car. So pretty exciting but now I want to make it more difficult for the self-driving car. We want to take it to level three which will. Oh here we go. A mistake. Sorry about that. I thought it was already one game. But you know it can still make some mistakes actually. We say you can probably see a constant war. Close to 0.1. There we go. And that's probably the mistake. But anyway it's doing a great job right now. So we will take it to level 3 and level three will be to draw some obstacles but some difficult obstacles to the car and the car will have to find its way to the downtown in the airport by avoiding the obstacles. So there will be obstacles full of sand of course but it will have to avoid them and finally goes to the airport and downtown.

SELF DRIVING CAR - LEVEL 3

So now the challenge is going to be to still do the round trips between the airport and the downtown. But this time by avoiding obstacles and we will do all the obstacles ourselves you can draw any difficulty of obstacles. I'll try not to be too tough with the car because I want to make it to level 4 but let's keep this challenging. All right. So as usual we're going to select all these codes and execute and then we go with level 3. So let's load our brains. Here we go, the brain is loaded and the car isn't around trips properly. And so now let's throw some obstacles. All right. So what can we do now? First let's roll something like this. OK. And then what we can do is draw other obstacles like this and then maybe something like this. Something like this. And something like this. Let's see what it does. All right. So now what it's going to do. OK. Avoiding this obstacle now avoids this one no mistake again. So still it has to learn it's still exploring avoiding this obstacle. Perfect. Very good. Is it going to avoid this one? Great. It did. And going downtown and now going back to the airport avoid obstacles. Great. Now is it going to avoid this one this time. And now we're still on the stage. It's OK. I'll get this sticker. Maybe something like this will be better. The car will understand more because right now it is being quite stubborn. All right. Still avoiding this obstacle it seems not to have any problem with this one. What kind of problem is that? Better now. You see I got thicker which means that the punishment was harder with a worse word. And now it managed to avoid it. And this one avoided as well. Perfect. Now we have a functional self-driving car as it seems. So we're watching this one again. Great. And now avoiding this one great still going on some sun but it's ok. It will be punished for that anyway. Avoiding this one. So sorry this one was totally useful But you know we can do something like this if you want. You know to get this even more challenging for the car. All right. And OK we can add a big tip here so that it doesn't cheat because it's still crossing the tip of the obstacle and we can do the same for the other tips of the other obstacles that we go there we go there we go. Now let's see what it does now. OK. There we go again trying to reach the airport now. OK. Perfect. So going around the obstacle is not trying to find the best path. But anyway the goal is to reach the two goals: the downtown and the airports. Then we can add some code to you know try to find the best path. But we definitely already have a soul train car. All right. Great. Great job. And there we go again. I still get you on the Simpsons so it's still in Spanish we can actually look at this core function which is here as you can see it gets the punishment and this corporation is actually decreasing with time.

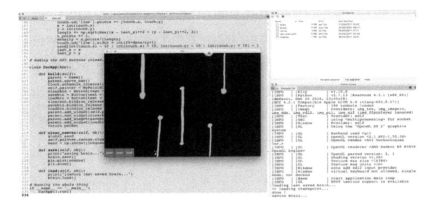

So that's because I got the obstacles figure and right now as you can see it's trying to avoid the tips of the obstacles more and more. It's doing them a better and better job as you can see you know it's going around faster now. Except for this one. But if we save again and look at this core function as you can see we see some kind of improvement here. But anyway the car is going to get better with time. But I think that right now we can say that level 3 is past because any way it manages to do the round trips between the airports and downtown by going around obstacles. And that's what we wanted. So yes maybe. Let's move on to level 4. Level 4 is going to be very challenging. I don't think we'll be able to pass level four but that will be the challenge of this model. You will have to change something in the code to pass level 4. It will either be something that has to do with the word or something that has to do with you knowing the strategy of the game or even something with the neural network or something with the D2 algorithm. Well you will look for it, you will do some research and you will try to get an even better card than this one that avoids any kind of obstacle that will never go into some sense or that will try to find the best way. The best path is the shortest path. So good luck with that. It's going to be excellent practice for you. And I can't wait to see your solutions. So now let's move on to level four. And this time it's going to be very very challenging.

SELF DRIVING CAR - LEVEL 4

So this time my goal will be to beat the self-driving car not the level four because I want to challenge you into improving the curves, improving the AI or maybe improving the strategy so that you can beat this challenge yourself. So I'm going to make a highly complex road that will still go from the airport to the downtown but maybe too complicated for the car to find its way. So that will be my challenge so I hope we can have fun with the challenging homework. So let's do this, let's approach this level. So let's select everything then let's load the brain and there we go. Now with the round trips between the airport and downtown. So it's going to take some time so I'm just going to put on some music and here we go with the road. And there we go. Here is the road. And as you can see the car seems to have a lot of trouble. So that's exactly what I wanted. It's you know doing these little round trips in the same part of the road. That's a problem. It doesn't find its way right now to the downtown. So how can we fix this? Do we need to change

334

the strategy or do we need to change the parameters of the neural networks that have changed the synopsis in the brain of the car? Do we need to do something with the words you know, maybe get a worse word when it's not finding the goal as it is the case right now. So I don't know how to find out. As you can see, the rewards are not very severe when it's not finding the goal. You know it's not getting closer to the goal. The reward is just minus 0.2. That's not a severe bad reward. You could try to decrease the reward even more like setting a reward equal to minus 0.5. Maybe that will work. And just throwing some suggestions to help you. So that's a change you can make with the word strategy. And then of course can make some other changes with your new network. So you know in this section we create the architecture of the new network. We choose to have 30 hidden neurons in one hidden layer.

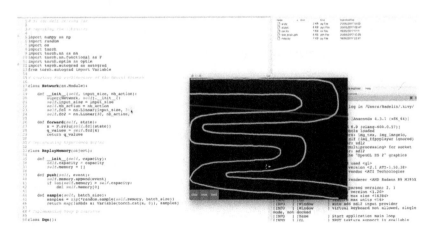

Maybe you can try to change the architecture by trying some more layers or some more hidden neurons I don't know. That's another suggestion for improvement. And then you can also try to change something in a deep learning algorithm or something you can move onto the course and find out about the other algorithms. Maybe there is another one that will manage to handle this situation. So good luck. I look forward to seeing your solutions try to draw that same road that's perfect. That's a really pretty exciting mystery. And if you want me to give you a hint or if you want me to explain quickly what the problem is. Well you can see that right here. When it reaches that point it's going back and that's because when it's reaching that point it's getting too far away from the goal which right now is downtown. You know when it's reaching that point if it goes further Well it will go further away from the goal. So that's why it's going back here. And so you have to change something in the code, something in the strategy to maybe punish it less when it's getting further away from the goal. Maybe that's the solution. I'm just throwing out some suggestions. I don't want to give you a solution too fast but that would be a really good exercise. And that's typically a problem that can be countered by engineers when they're making a self-driving car. But anyway I think that's a pretty cool enigma. So I hope you will have fun and before solving this homework maybe you can do another very efficient homework which would be simply to try to implement all this again. You know just implementing the exact same one will be excellent practice because so far you've just listened to my explanations but there is a huge difference between listening to something and trying to do the thing yourself. Oh oh did you see what happened. It just found its way. That's amazing. It's funny how it got out of it. But I'm sure there is a better strategy to get out of it more efficiently. And now it seems to be pretty good. Maybe I'm speaking too fast, maybe it's going to solve this. No. Here we go. It's getting stuck here again. That's pretty challenging for the car right. But I'm sure this can be solved.

PLAN OF ATTACK

And today's section we're going to tackle deep convolutional CULE learning. So we're taking deep learning too, even a further step, so we originally started to learn simple learning. Then we took that to deep learning and now we're taking too deep convolutional learning. So let's see what we're going to discuss in terms of intuition. Different sections are going to be quite quick. There's not much that we need to add as long as we're familiar with convolutional neural networks and we'll touch on this towards the end of this trial. So today in this section we're going to talk about deep relationship learning the intuition behind things and why it's so powerful why exactly it's so important to move away from deep Kule learning and why deep learning is just a basic building block where it's just a step for us on the postes to deep relationship learning and what kind of avenues deep can Lucian convolutional CULE learning opens up to what kind of avenues the knowledge opens up to and where it can be applied. We'll have some examples of that and then we'll talk about eligibility. Trace or end step learning is a very powerful addition to the whole concept of deep learning. And we'll talk about the intuition behind that. It's quite a complex topic but nevertheless we'll break down the intuition in quite simple terms and then I'll give you some additional references where you can read up about eligibility Tracy if you'd like to go into more detail but it is important for us to get the intuition down pat because we're going to be using that in practical terms because we're delving into much more complex topics now that we need to be add these extra or extra elements to our agents or to our learning algorithms so that they can actually handle these complex environments and navigate them successfully.

Plan of Attack

What we will learn in this section:

- Deep Convolutional Q-Learning Intuition
- Eligibility Trace (N-Step Q-Learning)

- Annex 2: Convolutional Neural Networks

And of course in this section because we're talking about convolutional neural networks it is highly advisable that you check out an x number to convolutional neural networks. Once again if you've done deep learning aitches at course then you're already familiar with this information so you can safely proceed with these projects on the deep emotional. If you haven't done the deep learning aitches of course then it's a great idea to look at convolutional neural networks and look at those intuitions. Charles there so you understand better how images are processed by neural networks in order to look for features and what's the whole convolutional layers are about pooling Lares the flattening layers and how all that works in order to come up with some parameters about that describe the environment or that describe that image and therefore we're going to be using those as inputs into our neural networks instead of that vector which we're talking about. But more on that in the next project. So if you haven't seen those controls yet we will advise you to check them out to get up to speed with or refresh knowledge on Cullerton illusional neural networks. All in all we've got an exciting section and as you can see what that many intuition Tournelles mean that you can. You'll be able to jump into the practical side of things very quickly.

www.ingramcontent.com/pod-product-compliance
Lightning Source LLC
La Vergne TN
LVHW051429050326
832903LV00030BD/2998